THE
LABOUR TRADE

THE LABOUR TRADE
Filipino Migrant Workers Around the World

First published 1987
Catholic Institute for International Relations
22 Coleman Fields, London N1 7AF, England
© CIIR 1987

British Library Cataloguing in Publication Data
The labour trade: Filipino migrant workers around the
    world.
    1. Alien labor, Philippine
    I. Catholic Institute for International Relations
    331.5'44   HD8716.5

    ISBN 0-946848-89-0
    ISBN 0-946848-22-X Pbk

Cover photo: Brenda Prince/FORMAT

Design by Jan Brown Designs
Printed in England by the Russell Press Ltd
Bertrand Russell House, Gamble Street,
Nottingham NG7 4ET

In the belly of the beast

How many years did we fight the beast together,
You in your violent way, in your troublous world,
I in my quiet way, with my songs of love?

Over the years we fought apart and together,
Scarring our lives, breaking our hearts
For the shining heart of a heartless world:
For the nameless multitudes in our beautiful land,
For the worker and the unemployed,
For the colored and the foreign born;

They are afraid, my brother,
They are afraid of our mighty fists, my brother,
They are afraid of the magnificence of our works,
my brother
They are even afraid of our songs of love,
my brother.

Song for Chris Mensalvas' birthday
by Carlos Bulosan,
Seattle, 1954

ACKNOWLEDGEMENTS

Migrants must usually remain silent, without names or roots in the economy which provides them with work. Many Filipinos, relatives of migrant workers or themselves abroad, have contributed to this story.

CIIR would like to thank all the organisations and individuals who have contributed to preparing this study, by telling their story, by drafting chapters or by demolishing errors.

In particular we would like to thank the staff of the Friends of Filipino Migrant Workers (Kaibigan) in Manila for their patient collaboration on this study, and for the sections they prepared on the Philippines, Asia and the Middle East, and on the economic cost of migration. Our thanks are due especially to Lea Aquino, Arnel de Guzman, Eileen Meneses, Conchita Posadas, Henry S. Rojas and Jorge Tigno. Kaibigan's research and publications programme and legal counselling and referral system clearly provides an invaluable service for migrant workers.

In addition we would like to thank the National Secretariat for Social Action (NASSA) in Manila for their assistance in the coordination of this project, the Mission for Filipino Migrant Workers in Hong Kong, which supplied us with much information about the situation in Hong Kong and Asia; the Commission for Filipino Migrant Workers in London for drafting the sections on Europe; Concerned Seamen of the Philippines and Paul Chapman of the Center for Seafarers' Rights, who prepared the chapter on seafarers; Ruben Cusipag for his draft on Canada; and Joel Rocamora from the Philippine Resource Center in Berkeley, who wrote the chapter on the United States.

We are most grateful to the Asia Partnership for Human Development, without whose generous grant this book could not have been written.

The Labour Trade will be published in the Philippines by Kaibigan and NASSA.

CONTENTS

Tables

Abbreviations

AMOSUP	Association of Marine Officers and Seamen's Union of the Philippines
APC	Alliance for Philippine Concerns
ASEAN	Association of South East Asian Nations
AWOC	Agricultural Workers' Organising Committee
BES	Bureau of Employment Services
EO 857	Executive Order 857
FAME	Filipino Association for Mariners' Employment
FFL	Filipino Federation of Labor
FLU	Filipino Labor Union
HSPA	Hawaii Sugar Planters' Association
IMF	International Monetary Fund
ILMS	Institute of Labor and Manpower Studies
KMU	May First Movement — *Kilusang Mayo Uno*
ILO	International Labour Organisation
ILWU	International Longshoremen's and Warehousemen's Union
ITF	International Transport Workers' Federation
MFA	Ministry of Foreign Affairs
MOLE	Ministry of Labor and Employment
NEDA	National Economic and Development Authority
NSB	National Seamen's Board
OCW	Overseas Contract Worker
OEDB	Overseas Employment Development Board
PNCC	Philippine National Construction Corporation
POCB	Philippine Overseas Construction Board
POCW	Processed Overseas Contract Worker
POEA	Philippines Overseas Employment Administration
PTGWU	Philippine Transport and General Worker's Union
UP	University of the Philippines

INTRODUCTION

'It really requires a lot of sacrifice. But what will happen to our family if my husband will not work abroad? Hunger!'

Wife of a contract worker

Throughout modern history young and able-bodied people from poor areas have migrated in search of work. In the 1970s and 1980s this economic exodus has taken place on a vast scale in Asia — promoted by governments for whom the labour trade has generated foreign currency and reduced the social pressures caused by unemployment. Literally millions of skilled and semi-skilled workers from Pakistan, Sri Lanka, Thailand, Malaysia, Indonesia, South Korea and the Philippines have travelled to the developed and capital-rich economies, giving years of their lives in exchange for a wage which they hope will give them and their families economic security.

For Filipinos, migrating to find work is not new. Many have sought 'greener pastures' abroad since the beginning of the century. Well over one million Filipinos have settled permanently in the United States and Europe, and the Philippines today is a leading Asian exporter of nurses, seafarers, and doctors.

Since the 1960s there has been a dramatic increase in the scale of the exodus, particularly for short-term contract workers. Between 1975 and 1985 well over one and a half million Filipinos travelled to find work abroad. This increase has occurred during one of the most dramatic periods of political and economic crisis in the country's turbulent history. About 70% of Philippine families now live below the government poverty line. Stiff repayment conditions imposed on the government by foreign lenders for a foreign debt of over US$25bn, make it unlikely that living standards will improve before the end of the decade. Widespread disenchantment with the regime of President Ferdinand E. Marcos, who for twenty years presided over a catastrophic decline in the country's economic performance, led to his fall in February 1986. The new government, led by President Corazon Aquino, faces enormous problems in re-establishing the economy and public confidence.

Under President Marcos, the government actively promoted the trade in

1

labour. It sought to take control over the profitable business of recruitment and passed laws which required Filipinos working abroad to remit as much as 80% of their earnings through Philippine banks, and which taxed them and the banks in the process. Between 1977 and 1983 Filipino migrants sent home more than US$3.5bn — about US$70 for every man, woman and child in the country. Migrant workers contribute more foreign exchange to the Philippine economy than traditional exports of sugar, minerals and wood products.

The great majority of those who go abroad are in the prime of their working lives. More than 80% are aged between 25 and 44. They are also educated: over 80% have completed high school, many have college or professional qualifications, and the great majority have at least one year's work experience. They are therefore among the country's most active and skilled people — a fact which raises fundamental questions about the real benefits of a trade which now affects the lives of almost every Filipino family.

Educating a child to high school level in the Philippines, for example, costs the equivalent of several thousand US dollars — and it costs even more to put someone through university. The total social investment in those who work abroad — a cost which is of course born by the Philippines rather than the receiving country — runs to millions of dollars.

Almost all the women who work abroad are single and make up the majority of the Filipino communities in Hong Kong, Japan, and Britain. The majority of men, on the other hand, are contract workers, 80% of whom are married. Most are working in the Middle East construction industry, and are separated for months or years from their wives and children.

The labour trade is about numbers — about unemployment statistics, wage rates and the costs of subsistence. At the centre, however, it is an individual experience lived by hundreds of thousands of families all over the Philippines, in all walks of life. This book describes their situation in different countries. We have tried to hint at the extraordinary variety of experience of those who have chosen the path of exile, who have dared to fly off into the unknown in search of work, and have so often made personal sacrifices in order to support their families back in the Philippines.

Exchange rates

	US$	Peso
Dec 1982	1	8.97
Dec 1983	1	13.84
June 1984	1	17.52
June 1986	1	20.78

(Figures from Daily Telegraph Information Unit, 28 Nov 1986)

PART 1
IN THE
PHILIPPINES

CARLOS REYES

1. FEELINGS OF LOSS

'Even the men cry on leaving and cling to their children at the airport. When the airplane lifted off, I felt as though my own body was being dislocated.'
A woman in Negros Occidental, 1981

The material well-being of many families has undoubtedly been improved because one or more family members have gone abroad to work. The country's economic crisis, increasingly acute since the late 1970s, makes it desperately hard for the majority of skilled and semi-skilled workers to support their children. Wages are currently little more than US$3 a day, and 30-40% of the population are thought to be underemployed or without work. No less than 70% of families live below the official poverty line. For this reason, emigration offers many the only hope of breaking out of the poverty trap.

Out of the poverty trap?
The jump in earnings may be colossal. A skilled construction worker might earn 1,500 pesos a month (US$75) in the Philippines, and more than US$500 per month in the Middle East.

Even a short walk through the streets of Philippine towns demonstrates the short-term individual returns of labour migration. Dotted among poor houses, built of board and scavenged construction materials, are brick-built

ISAGANI'S STORY

'Before overseas employment Ana and Isagani used to wonder how they could save because of their very small earnings. They aspired to build their own house and did not know whether this aspiration would find fulfilment. After she got married, Ana was only earning 8 Peso per day. She and Isagani were able to survive on that amount even when they already had two children. Their food only cost 15 peso per week, and their house rental was only 35 peso per month... When he transferred to a bigger company, he was earning 10 peso per day and the highest he received was only 14 peso per day. When Isagani moved again to another construction project, he was already earning 1,500 Peso per month. Isagani's earnings, however, were supplemented by Ana's earnings from her sari-sari store, her short-lived chicken business, and her buy and sell business. Despite their small earnings, Ana claimed that they were able to save some money.

When Isagani left for Algeria, however, they had more savings. On his first year, his basic salary was US$475. His overtime rate was 50% higher than the basic rate. Isagani used to work for around 12 to 15 hours so the overtime was really higher than the basic rate. On his second and third year, the basic rate went up to US$624 per month. He continued to have the same overtime arrangement and number of working hours.'

From: *The Effects of International Contract Labour* Vol. II, pp69-70

solid houses — all recently erected by migrants' families. They may not have access to piped drinking water, there will not be a public sewerage system, the streets themselves will be cramped, perhaps unpaved or partially flooded, but inside these houses will be a colour television set, a radio-cassette recorder or video system.

In addition to liberating the fortunate from the immediate threat of poverty, overseas earnings may permit parents to offer their children an education which they hope will free them permanently from economic need. Of those who are able to hold down overseas jobs for long enough to save, a high proportion invest their money first in building a home and then in educating their children. It is an ironic reflection on the sacrifices such parents make that the training their children receive may qualify them only to go abroad themselves. Even for those with professional skills, wages in the Philippines are low and there is chronic unemployment. A high proportion of Filipino contract workers are already college-educated — and most are doing jobs which bear no relationship to their professional or academic qualifications.

The cost to the family

Although there are material advantages to overseas migration, a high price is usually paid by the workers and their families. Homesickness and loneliness are perhaps the most serious challenge, for couples as well as for their children. The fact that workers frequently choose to do more than one tour abroad increases the strain. 'It was more painful and difficult the second time,' said one wife. 'Since we missed each other due to the long separation during his first stint, our togetherness was overwhelming when he came back. You know, the usual sweet nothings. Romantic moments. We didn't even quarrel. And then, he suddenly would have to leave again for the next working contract. Just when we were enjoying our togetherness. It really hurts.' 'When my husband was still here, he was unemployed,' declared another woman. 'But although we didn't have money and new clothes, the family was happy at Christmas. Now, no matter if we have... money and clothes for the kids, we are sad because he's not around. We're thinking about how he's doing abroad.'

Most workers and their families write very regularly, or talk to each other on the telephone, or send each other taped messages or photographs. 'My homesickness somehow disappears whenever I receive letters from you,' wrote one worker. 'It really feels good to at least have something to read upon returning to our barracks. Please write a longer letter next time...'

'Send pictures of the kids and, most especially, of yourself. Homesickness really strikes strong out here! My co-worker Betong is already crying and I just couldn't tease him because he might get angry. That's why you should write me more often, because, as you know me, I easily get homesick.'

Children may suffer even more. They 'cry a lot when they remember, especially at night. It's lucky enough if they don't ask about him every day.'

'You know what my eldest daughter did? She wore the T-shirt that her father used right before he left. All day long, that T-shirt was hanging on her neck while she was playing (...) My other child, who's only three years old, kept the slippers of her father in one corner. She gets angry whenever anyone touches them. They miss and long for their father; and they endlessly ask me when he is coming back.'

Some very young children even fail to recognise their father when he comes home or identify him with any male who comes to the house. 'When our Papa came home, my three year old sister, Jingjing didn't know who he was. She thought he was just a visitor, a stranger. She was even scared to come near him.' For parents, this can be a painful experience.

The risks

It is too soon to say whether the separation of families will cause any long-term changes in the close Philippine family structure. The partners of overseas workers certainly carry greater responsibilities than before, having to assume the roles both of household head and single parent.

'Sometimes, I find it difficult to decide whether I'll buy a certain thing or not. You know, such usual household decisions which used to be made by both the husband and wife.' 'Sometimes, it crosses my mind what if something unexpected happens to my children and I, now that we are left by ourselves? Say, what if a fire suddenly breaks out in the house?'

Most migrants' wives are especially worried that their children may fall

AMELITA'S HOME

A couple, without children and therefore more prosperous than most, declared that, before the husband worked abroad, 'Life used to be terribly difficult because often there was just enough money for food. (...) The first remitted earnings ... were used to defray household expenses. Later the family was able to buy a TV set, refrigerator, a sala set (furniture), a bed and a piece of land in Parian. They bought a 240-square meter lot for Peso 20,000 very recently (...). If the husband goes abroad again, they may be able to start constructing the house. From his earnings abroad, they were also able to improve the two houses in the lot of (wife) Amelita's mother. The house which they are occupying is now cemented and well-furnished(...) (They had) loaned money without interest to some friends who needed help, and gave money to relatives as well as saving for the future.'

From: *The Effects of International Contract Labour* Vol. II, pp290-291

sick while their husbands are away. Few families of moderate or low income in the Philippines have effective health insurance, and public health provision is particularly poor.

Above all, families worry about the health of those who are away — knowing well that life on the jobsite is harsh and often dangerous. Many workers avoid writing about the risks they run or the problems they experience. There are many accidents and workers are sometimes killed while they are abroad. In countries like Iran or Iraq, workers may find themselves in a war zone. Quite a number become destitute or are unable to get home because their company closes down without taking care of them. The families may remain in complete ignorance of such disasters, or only learn about them long afterwards.

In one instance, for example, the husband of a schoolteacher from Iloilo went to Saudi Arabia on a two-year contract as a general mechanic. He caught hepatitis and subsequently died. His wife did not learn until some time after his funeral that he had been transferred from his former skilled work to an unskilled construction job, and that he had not received proper medical attention during his illness. Nor were the family informed until afterwards that the husband had been sick for several months before his death. Only with considerable difficulty, after seeking help in Manila from the advice group Kaibigan, were the family able to claim the death and other benefits which were due to them.

There are numerous similar stories.

Debt and fraud

Though the government has set a legal limit on the costs which workers can legally be charged during their recruitment, in practice the expense may vary widely. One report estimated in 1981 that 'the total cost of sending (a migrant worker) abroad was Peso 7,272 — or Peso 7,768 for land-based and

MANG ABE'S STORY

'In his effort to avail himself of an overseas contract, Mang Abe experienced many pitfalls. Although he was able to go abroad, there was a breach of contract on the part of the agency. They were sent home after only eight months, while the contract guaranteed them employment for two years. Thus, he and four other co-workers have filed a suit against the agency and the Ministry of Labor and Employment. Each is asking for an amount of Peso 56,000 which is equivalent to the pay they would have earned in two years.(....)

Prior to his departure for Saudi Arabia, he was asked to sign a blank piece of paper(.....). Because of this, he had doubts about going abroad, but went anyway. He found out that it was stipulated there that in case he loses the job he was hired for, he would become only a driver earning much less than he had hoped for. Drivers are not paid that much there. There was also a statement regarding remittances which the respondent still could not quite figure out.

Another problem he mentioned was when a recruitment agency operator duped him and his friend and got away with the money they paid him. He thought that when they found this person in 1979, he had hit the jackpot already because all those who were with him there were former OCW's. Thus, he thought there was less chance of getting victimised. But he ended up losing Peso 1,700 in the process. The money actually came from a mortgage. He mortgaged the land in San Cristobal for Peso 3,000 and it was from this money that he took his expenses. Still he said that he was luckier than the others who lost a much larger amount of money.'

From: *The Effects of International Contract Labour* Vol. II, pp297-298.

Peso 6,592 for sea-based workers'.[1] In the majority of cases this money was borrowed from relatives and friends or drawn from personal saving; very few pawned their land or borrowed from private moneylenders or banks.[2] 'One wife reported borrowing Peso 7,000 from a friend without any interest (...).' Another informant claimed that 'For her husband, who went to Iran in 1977, they borrowed Peso 5,000 at 20% interest and their lot served as collateral (...) For one son who left on a one year contract in Iran in 1980, the family borrowed Peso 25,000 (...) For another son who had a 12-month contract in Kuwait in 1982, they spent Peso 20,000.[3]

In some cases these sums amount to well over the total annual wage of the person going abroad. Families seem to accept them because, provided the job works out, the debt can eventually be repaid.[4]

This is not true for all, of course. Some pay more than two or three times the average outlay for securing a job overseas, and remain locked in debt even though they are receiving quite substantial sums in remitted earnings.

The most difficult economic period occurs just after the migrants depart, because remittances do not usually start coming in for about three months.

CARLOS REYES

In addition, there are often delays in payment.

In one instance, families of employees of the Philippine National Construction Corporation (PNCC) complained about delays and irregularities in their remittances. A backlog of six months had developed, making it virtually impossible for them to make ends meet. Many became hopelessly indebted to neighbours, local shops, relatives, and friends. The case was only solved when the families organised themselves and pressed collectively for the money owed them.

In other cases, workers have taken direct action themselves when they have learnt their remittances have not been paid. One Italian company, for example, took the precautionary step of calling together the wives of its employees 'to tell them to refrain from telling their husbands abroad about delayed remittances because this information received by a few husbands abroad led to a strike among the first batch of workers'.[5]

It should be appreciated that debt, once incurred, is extremely difficult to clear in the Philippines, because the standard level of interest set by private moneylenders is 20% per month. If remittances are delayed for any reason, or the overseas worker is not paid — or, as frequently happens, he returns and is unable to find another job — debts can become crippling.

Not all companies or agencies claim high fees or take bribes when arranging jobs for clients or employees. Some companies are known to be scrupulously fair — and attract well-qualified applicants for this reason. Nevertheless, outrageously high charges, corruption and bribery are so common that they are taken for granted.

Because they have access to cash, migrants' families also come under pressure from neighbours and relatives. Many contribute to their churches and local associations. A number also lend money — at interest or without interest — to people who come to them for help. The visible inequalities of income which are apparent in communities in which significant numbers take overseas work is almost certainly a cause of jealousy and tension. Many of those interviewed showed sensitivity to criticism that they might be acting 'above themselves' and made attempts to reduce hostility of this kind. Jealousy is no doubt also one cause of the frequent rumours of extra-marital affairs which circulate around the wives of migrant workers. Though these appear to have little foundation in fact, more than one husband has raced back from the Middle East or, on his return home, physically assaulted his wife because rumours that she was being unfaithful had reached him abroad.

For the individual, emigration may be a solution to some of the most pressing problems of poverty — though it is achieved at the cost of prolonged separation.

Against this, however, emigration reduces the number of skills contained within the community as a whole, increases economic inequalities and is not likely to create a pool of productive capital from which the entire community will eventually benefit. In almost all cases, migrants' families spend their cash first on food and the basic necessities, then on housing, and finally on educating their children in the hope that they at least will find well-paid and secure jobs.

Even the educated and professional workers are now leaving the Philippines, however, since they cannot find jobs inside the country. Education itself has become a qualification to travel, and the phenomenon of migration — initially declared by government to be a temporary response to a short-term need — threatens to become institutionalised from generation to generation.

2. HISTORY

'Spurred on by the agent's stories of gold and easy riches awaiting eager hands, the uninformed labourers are easily duped into mortgaging their properties... to pay their passage (to Hawaii).'

Filipinos began migrating to find work from the beginning of this century, in response to the demand for agricultural workers on the United States mainland and its colony of Hawaii. They left a nation devastated by two wars of national liberation, against Spain and against the United States. In 1901 the United States had established a new colonial order, replacing that of Spain which had been in occupation since the middle of the 16th century. The new government promoted 'free trade' policies which caused the Philippines to be flooded by American surplus commodities, and encouraged the cultivation of cash crops (tobacco, coconut, pineapple, sugarcane).

Compounded by the after-effects of a war which had decimated the population, these colonial demands undermined the traditional subsistence economy. Production was geared to export and not for domestic consumption, causing widespread poverty in the countryside and stimulating labour migration inside the country as well as abroad.[1]

Working for the United States (1900-1946)

The first contract workers went in 1906 to Hawaii, which at the beginning of the century was being transformed into a plantation economy. As rich 'haoles' (foreigners of European descent) occupied more and more of the land, the peasant farmers were dispossessed and began selling their labour as plantation workers. But the demand for labour could not be satisfied by Hawaiians, who were weakened by poverty and by new diseases being brought to the island. As a result many Hawaiians died. The companies therefore imported labour from abroad.

They recruited in China, Japan, Portugal, and Korea. Smaller groups of workers came from the continental United States, Mongolia, Puerto Rico, Spain, Italy, Poland, Austria, Germany, Norway, Russia, Siberia, and Oceania. The first group of Filipinos arrived on December 20, 1906 — a group of 15 Ilocano men assigned to work on the Olaa sugar plantation.[2]

Migrant workers for the Hawaiian plantations were generally recruited on contract, a system which was officially abolished in 1900 (when the Hawaiian islands became a United States territory) but which in fact continued for many years. The workers signed written contracts drawn up by the planter or his agents which specified the length and terms of employment. Under such contracts, workers had no channels to express their grievances, nor could they leave their jobs; under Hawaiian laws, a breach of contract could be punished by detention or even beating. In early years, when most of the workers could not read or write, contracts often included no provision for return passage to the Philippines.

The first major recruiting drive in the Philippines was undertaken in 1908 by the Hawaii Sugar Planters' Association (HSPA), which began recruiting

in the Philippines and in Puerto Rico because both countries were colonies of the US. As a result Filipinos and Puerto Ricans, unlike Japanese and other groups of foreign workers, were not subject to American immigration laws and were convenient sources of cheap labour to Hawaii.

Initially, Filipino labourers refused to take contracts. But by increasing the financial incentives and resorting to deceptive methods of recruitment, the HSPA brought very large numbers of Filipinos into Hawaii after 1909, and more than 120,000 had been contracted by 1934.

The methods used by HSPA recruiters were described by a Filipino provincial official:

> In addition...to the (HSPA) man in charge of general recruiting, there is one who goes from town to town, showing a movie of life in Hawaii. One scene shows the handing out of checks. The movie is free and is usually shown in the town plaza, so that everyone has a chance to see it. This and ordinary conversation, rather than advertising are the most important agents of (their) propaganda... Spurred on by the agent's stories of gold and easy riches awaiting eager hands, the uninformed laborers are easily duped into mortgaging their properties or borrowing from their relatives and thus getting sufficient funds to pay their passage. Many of the labor

15

recruiters received this money and then disappeared, or say the money has been misappropriated by someone else to whom it was entrusted. Several prosecutions have been initiated by the government but they were conducted lifelessly and so far have failed to stop the practices complained of.[3]

Most of these recruits were farmers with little or no educational background. The majority were male (87%) and came from the provinces of Ilocos Norte, Ilocos Sur, Cebu and Pangasinan, which accounted for 72% of all overseas Filipino workers between 1916 and 1928. The proportion who came from islands in the Visayas — notably Cebu and Negros — dropped off in the 1920s, because the HSPA built about 35 sugar mills, most of which were situated in Negros. By 1928, Visayan workers, who had composed the majority of early immigrants, only represented 5% of Filipino arrivals and HSPA agents shifted their recruitment efforts to the provinces of northern Luzon, particularly Ilocos, which supplied over half the workers recruited between 1925 and 1928. At this time (1929), Filipinos accounted for 18% of the entire population of Hawaii.

As employment opportunities dried up in Hawaii, many Filipinos were again forced to migrate out of the sugar plantations. More than 41% of the Filipinos living there either returned to the Philippines or went on to the US mainland, where the majority followed the harvest trail, picking fruit, asparagus and other crops in season, or worked in the fish canning industry in Nova Scotia.[4]

The Philippine Independence (Tydings-McDuffie) Act of 1934 granted the country commonwealth status and recreated Filipino citizenship. From that date Filipinos were considered under US immigration law to be aliens. Their entry to Hawaii and the US mainland was restricted to a quota of just 50 persons per year.

Working for the First World (1946-1960s)

After Japan's defeat in World War II, South-East and East Asian countries were burdened by the heavy task of rebuilding their economies, which had been shattered by the war.

The Philippines had suffered more than most. Manila was the most damaged city in Asia and the country saddled with a large debt (most of which was owed to foreign owners of pre-war public works bonds). The war damages granted in 1946 were far less than needed for adequate reconstruction. When the United States granted 'independence' on July 4, 1946, the country remained politically dependent, and its neo-colonial economy still relied primarily upon agricultural exports — a situation which has not changed since.

Immediately after the second world war, in 1946, the HSPA and the Pineapple Growers' Association was able to recruit 7,000 Filipinos to work in Hawaii, by taking advantage of a loophole in the Tydings-McDuffie Act which permitted companies to employ foreign labour when there was a demonstrated labour shortage. Nevertheless, after the national origin quota system was introduced in the same year, Filipinos could no longer enter the United States. Between 1946 and 1965, only 100 Filipinos per year were permitted to enter the US; most of the immigrants during this period were therefore relatives of earlier immigrants, or members of the United States armed forces, who were given preference.

The American armed forces were generally an important employer for Filipinos.

> The American military as well as independent contractors hired Filipinos for war reconstruction work on the Pacific Islands like Wake, Guam, and Okinawa. With the outbreak of the Korean War and later the Vietnam War, the American military specifically sought Filipinos for work on construction sites. In the latter case, the demand was so great that recruitment offices were set up in Manila. At this time, local employers complained about the outflow of skilled labour to Vietnam and, for the first time, the Philippine government formulated a specific policy to ensure the inflow of overseas remittances.[5]

Filipino contract workers were also employed in British North Borneo (Sabah) in the late 1950s and in Thailand and Malaysia in the 1960s. The Philippine government's claim to Sabah caused Malaysia to expel Filipino workers from East Malaysia in 1969. Projects in Vietnam involving Filipino labour also ended after 1972.

In the later 1960s Canada and the United States relaxed their immigration rules and there was again a surge of Filipino migration to the Western hemisphere. The 1965 US Immigration Act abolished the national origin quota system and very many Filipinos took advantage of it to emigrate. The majority were skilled professionals — doctors, nurses, engineers, dental technicians and dieticians.

Many also went to Europe which, like the United States and Canada, faced shortages of labour at a time of rapid economic growth. In Britain, France, Italy and other European countries, tens of thousands of Filipinos found jobs as hotel workers, hospital workers, personal maids and nurses. Most of those who emigrated to Europe were also skilled and had experience as teachers or professionals. Where they were permitted to do so, a high proportion settled and today form permanent communities. Where this was not possible, as in France and Germany, many have been forced to live for long periods in semi-clandestinity.

It was also during this period that a large number of Filipinos found employment in the international shipping industry, which grew rapidly during the 1960s and 1970s. Although skilled and relatively well trained, the majority of Filipino sailors and officers are today employed on ships sailing under 'flags of convenience', which frequently fail to implement minimum wage or safety standards.

The Middle East, Asia and Africa (1972-present)

Following the declaration of martial law in 1972, the Marcos government

17

played an increasingly active role in regulating and promoting the export of Filipino workers.

Officially, the Marcos government's view was that:

The export of manpower will be allowed only as a temporary measure to ease underemployment and will increasingly be restrained as productive domestic employment opportunities are created. This will ensure the availability of talents and skills needed to raise production efficiency in all sectors of the economy.[6]

In practice, however, labour export was energetically promoted. The oil boom in the Middle East provided jobs for thousands of construction workers and new markets for Filipino labour were sought out in Asia and Africa. Little account was taken of its long term social and economic impact. It was used as a short-term measure to alleviate the economic crisis which gripped the country from the late 1970s, causing high unemployment and widening the balance of payments deficit. In his relentless quest for foreign currency, Marcos adopted more and more repressive social and economic controls over migrants and the number of contract workers going abroad in this period increased very sharply. By 1983 it had reached its peak of 434,207 overseas workers, representing more than 2% of the entire Philippine labour force.

Table 1: Geographical Distribution of Processed Overseas Contract Workers (POCW) 1975–1983

				Distribution as a percentage of the total			
Year	Africa	Asia	Europe	Middle East	Oceania	The Americas	Trust Terri.
1975	2.7	33.7	25.3	12.4	4.4	18.4	3.1
1976	2.5	28.1	15.1	40.6	0.7	11.3	1.7
1977	1.4	14.4	6.8	70.1	0.4	6.2	0.7
1978	2.6	19.6	2.5	67.6	0.2	6.6	1.0
1979	1.2	13.6	0.7	79.1	0.3	4.0	0.9
1980	1.0	11.3	0.5	83.9	0.1	2.2	0.9
1981	1.0	9.6	0.5	87.0	0.1	1.0	0.7
1982	0.4	12.4	0.6	85.1	0.3	1.5	0.5
1983	0.6	10.7	0.8	85.1	0.5	1.5	0.8

Sources: Philippine Overseas Employment Administration 1984 Annual Report, p.32. Fr Anthony Paganoni (ed), *Migration from the Philippines*, Scalabrinian Fathers (Manila), 1984, p.20.

The situation today

Today the market for migrant workers is shrinking, particularly as a result of the rapid decline in the Middle East construction industry. Table 1 shows the striking shift which took place in the geographical distribution of migrant workers. Although scattered today in 124 countries worldwide, the vast majority of Filipino overseas workers are in the Middle East, particularly in the Kingdom of Saudi Arabia. In 1983 85% of the 434,207 Filipinos working overseas were employed in the Middle East.

During the period covered by the table the number of Filipinos working in Africa doubled, the number in Asia tripled. Numbers decreased only in Europe, where stringent immigration controls frequently made it impossible to find legal employment. In Asia, most of the migrants are women; 95% of those in legal work are domestic helpers.

In Africa there are about 15,000 Filipinos scattered over Nigeria, the Sudan, Ethiopia and Kenya — they are even to be found in South Africa's bantustans — working as teachers, doctors, economists, administrators and engineers. In Western Europe, where about 117,000 live, the majority work as domestic helpers, hotel chambermaids or nurses. In the United States, Filipinos are now the second largest recognised minority, after the Mexicans.

Under Marcos the programme may well have temporarily eased underemployment and it certainly provided much needed foreign exchange. It was not however matched by the promised creation of domestic employment opportunities. The declining overseas job market will undoubtedly increase unemployment as contract workers return and no new contracts are available, and foreign exchange earnings, which in 1984 amounted to US$950m, will consequently be reduced. For President Aquino the legacy of Marcos' 'manpower export programme' can only add further pressure to an already critical situation.

3. GOVERNMENT REGULATION OF LABOUR MIGRATION

'Illegal recruiters are not responsible for all the cases of corruption or injustice. Legal statistics show that licensed and illegal recruiters are prosecuted in almost equal numbers.'

Effects of International Contract Labour

From 1915 to 1974, successive governments regulated the movement of labour abroad through Act 2486. This act required recruiters to pay a tax to the national government and to the authorities in provinces where they operated. It prohibited the recruitment of minors under 18 years of age, without parental permission, or ethnic minorities for exhibition purposes, and obliged recruiters to ensure migrants were provided a passage home at the end of their contract, if they fell ill or were injured.

A number of administrative orders were later introduced but the situation did not alter fundamentally until 1974, when the New Labor Code (1974) was announced. This created, within the Ministry of Labor and Employment (MOLE), three government agencies charged with developing, promoting, regulating, and implementing a comprehensive overseas employment programme. They were the Overseas Employment Development Board (OEDB), the National Seamen's Board (NSB) and the Bureau of Employment Services (BES). The OEDB was the government placement agency for land-based workers, the NSB for seafarers. The BES was responsible for the regulation and supervision of private employment agencies.

Office of Philippines Overseas Employment Administration, Manila

22

Then on May 1, 1982, President Marcos reorganised the Ministry of Labor again, and created a single body to take responsibility for matters relating to labour migration — the Philippine Overseas Employment Administration (POEA). The government wanted to streamline procedures and coordinate the export of labour more efficiently. The POEA's brief was defined as:

The promotion and development of employment opportunities abroad ... in cooperation with relevant government agencies and entities as well as representative groups from the private sector, through organised market promotion activities and services which shall include among others, the following:

a) a comprehensive manpower marketing strategy and despatch of marketing missions abroad for this purpose;

b) to develop and promote programs or arrangements that would encourage the hiring of Filipinos in organised or corporate groups as well as government-to-government arrangements;

c) to promote Filipino manpower through advertising in appropriate media overseas.[1]

The POEA is responsible for negotiating and managing contracts signed with other governments for Filipino workers, and requires all agencies acting on behalf of foreign governments to clear their applications for recruitment through its offices.

The Overseas Employment Development Board, and the POEA, have

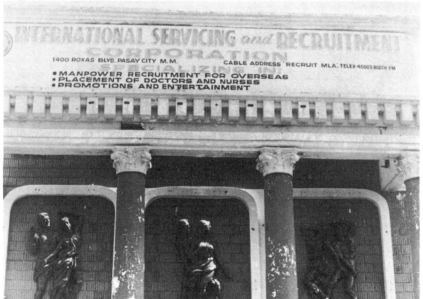

Recruiting agency, Manila

23

promoted the export of Filipino labour energetically. Government ministers have regularly canvassed abroad on behalf of the programme. In 1982, for example, President Marcos undertook a marketing mission to Saudi Arabia, while his Minister of Labor visited Italy, Japan and Singapore. Since then, official missions have gone to the Middle East, the United States, the Pacific region and Europe. The government also used modern marketing techniques, like the 'Direct Mailer Campaign', to contact more than 500 current and prospective international clients.

Private contractors

In the early 1970s, when the OEDB was created, the government intended to suppress labour recruitment by the private sector. In the reorganisation of 1974, the government declared that it would phase out private overseas recruitment of Filipino workers, and expand the recruitment operations of

DUPED BY FAKE AGENTS

Seventeen of the 45 workers victimised by illegal recruiters, who promised them jobs in Malaysia, went aground on a coral reef off Tawi Tawi. They were rescued by the Philippine Marine Task Force, after their boat was stranded on their way to Sabah.(...)

Seven of the workers landed in Borneo but were arrested by Borneo police for illegal entry. They were jailed for nine days and later deported to the Philippines.

The remaining nine were able to go back somehow to recount their ordeal to Ministry of Defense authorities.

These 45 workers were illegally recruited in Pangasinan, Nueva Ecija and La Union. They related how they had to sell their work animals or tracts of land, or borrowed money at usurious interest just to be able to pay 5,000 pesos each to the recruiters for jobs in Malaysian plantations.

Meanwhile, eight Filipinas travelling on fake visas and airline tickets were deported by Singapore authorities, even before they could leave the airport.

The girls pointed to a certain Luz Esguerra Tan as the recruiter who had asked the applicants for 8,500 pesos each for passport and visa, and an additional 300 pesos each at the airport to facilitate their MIA exit.

From: *Pinoy Overseas Chronicle*, 1984

---

the OEDB, which would eventually take over all overseas employment functions. The New Labor Code declared that:

> ...no new application for a license to operate...shall be entertained ... The Department of Labor shall, within four (4) years from the effectivity of this Code, phase out the operation of all private fee charging employment agencies, including those engaged in the overseas recruitment and placement of individuals for personnel services or to make up the crew of a vessel.

The Code permitted applicants for overseas jobs to be charged fees and for the first time obliged workers to remit a proportion of their earnings, barred companies from hiring workers directly in the Philippines, and prohibited travel agents from recruiting at all.

The policy was never to be implemented. It met strong opposition from the private sector, which — with reason — challenged the OEDB's ability to manage the rapidly expanding foreign demand for Filipino labour. By 1978, placements had risen by 150% and government departments were clearly overstretched. From 1978 private contractors were again encouraged to recruit and the terms of Presidential Decree 1412 removed almost all restrictions on their activities.

Between 1975 and 1982, in fact, the private sector placed 600,000 workers, or 63% of total overseas placements, and in 1983 alone increased its turnover by 52%. From 15 in 1975, the number of registered private recruiters swelled to 554 in 1980, to 815 in 1982, and to 1023 by the end of 1983, an increase during the period of 6,700%. Of these 579 were fee-charging private employment agencies, 231 were construction contractors, 164 were manning agents and 49 service contractors.

The government's 'Corporate Export Strategy' (Letter of Instruction 852, May 1, 1979) aimed to group contracts for Filipino workers. MOLE and the Philippine Overseas Construction Board (POCB) granted tax and other incentives to contractors involved in this scheme. The result was to greatly enhance the participation of the private sector in the lucrative employment and contracting business.

Its share of the international market also increased, particularly in the Middle East; the value of contracts rose from $359m in 1979, to $922m in 1982. The number of companies involved rose even faster, from 26 in 1977 to 231 in 1983. Most were subcontractors, who hired and supplied labour to the principal contractors. This was an extremely lucrative operation, because many companies paid much lower wages than the contract price had assumed. According to one writer,

The difference between the subcontract supply price and what the Filipino construction company pays the workers they supply can be significant. It is an extremely profitable operation and in itself explains the considerable pressure the construction companies brought to bear on the government to prevent non-restricted recruitment of construction workers. It merits mention that few Filipino construction companies hold prime contracts in the Middle East.[2]

Hiring and Rights

Before 1981, private recruitment agencies had no right to charge direct or indirect fees from the worker or from employers. In that year, Parliamentary Bill 4531 (known as the Omnibus Employment Bill) amended the legal definition of private recruitment agencies and effectively allowed them to collect fees. In 1983, POEA went a step further, and formally permitted private recruitment agencies to charge fees.

A maximum documentation fee was set, ranging from 700 to 900 pesos, and the placement and documentation fee was increased to a maximum of 5,000 pesos. This sum was meant to cover all placement and documentation fees, and all the costs of services such as trade/skill testing, medical examinations, passport, visas, clearances, inoculation, airport terminal fees, travel taxes, legal costs etc.

In addition, recruits for both licensed agencies and authority holders were covered by a 20,000 peso insurance policy, the premium for which was paid equally by the employer and worker. This bond was designed to ensure, for the employer, that the labourer would work as expected.

Philippine legislation includes many clauses protecting the rights of

NICANOR'S MISFORTUNE

Nicanor found out that he had to pay 3,500 pesos to the company in order to obtain an overseas job as a construction helper. This did not deter him from pursuing his wish because he immediately informed his mother that he needed some money. The family was able to raise the amount by putting together the little they had saved plus the money his two brothers, who are both overseas contract workers, had donated. In the end, Nicanor was able to board the plane for a construction jobsite in Iraq on July 15, 1981.

Nicanor's misfortunes started as soon as he reached Iraq. There, he found out that his group of Filipino workers did not have any contract with the construction firm they were supposed to work for. They were being asked to sign a piece of paper which the foreigners claimed was a contract, but they refused to do so because it was written in Arabic. Meanwhile they continued to work for two months without pay under the supervision of heavily armed men. They then decided to stage a strike that dragged on for another four months... During the strike he washed dishes in a restaurant to earn some money. He even revealed that he approached a number of Filipinos he saw in the streets of Iraq and asked them for money. After four months, the strikers approached the representative of the company to make a deal with him. They wanted to be flown back to the Philippines in exchange for their promise that no case would be filed against the recruiting agency. He finally came home penniless from his six month ordeal (...). Three weeks later, he received word that the Ministry of Labor had revoked the operating license of the company he had worked for and had closed down the firm. His family never got back any portion of the 3,500 pesos they paid the recruiter.

From: *The Effects of International Contract Labour*, Vol II, p.93.

Filipino overseas contract workers. The *New Rules and Regulations* of the POEA (Book 1, Rule 1) state, for example, that the POEA's policy is to 'afford protection to Filipino overseas contract workers and their families, promote their interests and safeguard their welfare'.

On paper, the Ministry of Labor has established wage and compensation standards, grievance machinery and dispute settlement procedures, auxiliary services such as a Welfare Fund for Workers, Pre-Departure Seminars, a Labor Assistance Center, and labour centres in host countries.

The reality is frequently very different, as even government officials have been obliged to recognise.

In 1979, the Philippine Task Force on Illegal Recruitment was able to file 1,479 cases and this is estimated to be only 10% of actual incidents. In 1983 Labor Deputy Minister Willie Villarama said in a television interview that of the 4,000 cases reported to his office (he is also part of the Task Force on Illegal Recruitment), 50% were perpetrated by licensed agencies.[3]

There are numerous forms of fraud. Outrageously high fees may be charged. Recruiters may ask workers to pay for services, such as air fares, for which they have already been paid by the employer. Workers may be expected to sign two contracts — one of which offers excellent wages and approved conditions of work and the other, the applied contract, much lower wages. Very many agencies take bribes and 'overlook' clients who do not offer money. Workers have been sent to quite fictitious work sites and they have even been dumped in another part of the Philippines rather than the US or Saudi Arabia.

When they arrive in a country, workers can find that the jobs which await them are not those for which they applied. Overtime which they work may not be paid, their remittances may be delayed by the recruiting agency, and agreed welfare allowances, repatriation agreements or health provisions may not be available. Instead of the 5,000 pesos which is the maximum workers are expected, by law, to pay for a job, an average of 6,000-10,000 pesos is required — and many pay far more.

Remittances: Executive Order 857

Like migrant workers from many other countries, Filipinos working abroad send very large amounts of their income home, to support their families. Frequently, they skimp on their own needs to do so. The government has always seen these earnings as a valuable source of foreign currency, and several edicts have been passed which encourage or require Filipinos to remit their savings through the Philippine banking system.[4]

The acute financial crisis which struck the government in the early 1980s caused it to introduce even more stringent controls. The Central Bank Governor declared, in 1983, that:

> Tapping the remittance of Filipino workers would be the most immediate and obvious means by which the country could improve her BOP (balance of payments) position which was estimated to be US$1bn in the red last year.

Executive Order 857 was therefore introduced in 1983 to achieve this purpose.

EO 857, which became effective on February 1 of that year, makes it 'mandatory for every Filipino contract worker abroad to remit regularly a portion of his foreign exchange earnings to his beneficiary in the Philippines through the Philippine banking system'.[5] It applied to sailors, who were required to remit 80% of their earnings; workers of Filipino contractors and construction companies (70%); doctors, engineers, nurses and other professional workers whose contracts provide for free board and lodging (70%); all other professional workers whose employment contracts did not provide for free board and lodging (50%); domestic and other workers

(50%); all other workers who did not fall within the above categories (50%). Excluded from EO 857 were: contract workers whose immediate family were living with them, provided they were not also contract workers, Filipino servicemen in US defence installations, emigrants and Filipino employees of the United Nations.

Before departure, workers were required to sign an undertaking pledging to comply with EO 857. Government agencies subsequently checked on their performance, requiring them to produce a confirmed bank remittance form, an authenticated certificate of payment from the employer or from a bank, or an official receipt from the Central Bank or a post office.

Workers who failed to remit the required amount have been subject to penalties.

The Ministry of Foreign Affairs (MFA) shall not extend or renew the passport of any contract worker unless proof of his compliance with the mandatory remittance requirement is submitted. The MOLE shall not approve the renewal of employment contracts (...) unless proof of remittance of foreign exchange earnings is submitted. Workers who fail to comply 'shall be suspended or excluded from the list of eligible workers for overseas employment'.[6]

The dollar remittance system has undoubtedly benefited the Philippine government. Since 1983 it has helped to keep the economy afloat. Between 1978 and 1984, the Philippine government was able to draw upon US$2.38bn from remittances alone — a figure which does not include money transferred through the black market and money courier systems.

EO 857 provoked widespread protest among Filipino workers in Europe, the United States, Hong Kong and the Philippines. It imposed, in authoritarian fashion, a very heavy burden on many migrants, and in doing so overrode some of their basic rights. A declaration criticising EO 857 was made public in Hong Kong in January 1985, supported by organisations representing Filipino women workers. In it, they declared that Filipino migrant workers do not oppose remitting money — 'On the contrary, this is precisely the reason, the foremost consideration, why we were forced to work abroad' — but they strongly opposed the government's intrusive control over how they spent what they earned, the inefficient and expensive banking transfer system, and finally the denial of their basic rights according to the Philippine constitution and international law, which include the right to freedom of travel, the right to work and earn a livelihood, and the right to enter freely into a contract.[7]

The International Labour Organisation (ILO) in Geneva has also criticised Executive Order 857, and described it as 'incompatible with Article 6 of ILO Convention No.95' on the Protection of Wages. This is a Convention which the Philippines has ratified, and which states 'Employers shall be prohibited from limiting in any manner the freedom of the worker to dispose of his wages.'

On May 1, 1985, President Marcos, as a result of this international pressure, repealed the punitive measures of EO 857, when he issued a new Executive Order (1020): though tamed, however, EO 857 retained its mandatory remittance provisions.

Since coming to power in February 1986 President Aquino has set in motion a plan to set up welfare centres for Filipino workers in different parts of the world. But, as yet she has made no fundamental changes in either the legislation governing basic rights of migrant workers and their remittances, nor in the controlling bodies.

President Aquino has expressed a desire to 'put people first' in her policies. In the case of the 'manpower export programme', she is faced with a dilemma of wanting on the one hand to respect the basic rights of the Filipino people but on the other needing the foreign exchange to service the country's US$26bn debt.

This presents her with a serious challenge which needs to be addressed in the context of any overall economic recovery programme.

PART 2
ABROAD

4. THE UNITED STATES

'The mockery of it all is that Filipinos are taught to regard Americans as our equals. Adhering to American ideals, living American life, these are contributory to our feelings of equality. The terrible truth in America shatters the Filipino's dreams of fraternity.'

Carlos Bulosan

Americans have played a more powerful role in the Philippines over the past century than any other people except Filipinos themselves. Together with British commercial interests, American traders financed the development of Philippine export agriculture in the 19th century. The United States then controlled the Philippines as a colony during most of the first half of this century. Since independence in 1946, it has continued to play a dominant role in Philippine political and economic life.

Throughout this century the Philippine education system has followed an American model. American English is still the primary language of instruction in high schools and universities. Even eating habits are heavily Americanised.

Today, neo-colonial relations between the US and the Philippines continue to influence the character of the Filipino community in the United States, helping to determine the growth of the US Filipino community, its economic role, its political character and even its social dynamics.

For the majority of Filipinos, 'going abroad' still means going to the US. Several hundred thousand have applied for immigrant visas, and there is always a queue of several hundred Filipino visa applicants in front of the US embassy in Manila. More than 80% of Filipino emigrants between 1965 and 1974 went to the US, and it is still the preferred destination even though a higher proportion are now going to Canada and Australia.

History

The first large group of Filipinos to come to the United States were peasant contract workers recruited to work in Hawaii's sugar plantations. Between 1906 and 1946, some 125,000 Filipinos came to Hawaii. In 1908, only 141 (0.3% of the workforce) worked in the plantations. By 1920, 30% (13,000) of plantation workers were Filipino. By 1932, Filipinos had become the majority of the workforce (70%).

Most of those who came to Hawaii were farmers, recruited by the Hawaii Sugar Planters Association (HSPA) from the Ilocano provinces of Ilocos Norte, Ilocos Sur, Abra, and La Union, where land scarcity drove large numbers to leave the region. The Cebuano-speaking provinces of Cebu, Bohol, and Negros Oriental contributed the second largest group.

Takaki writes:

> On the plantations, all of the migrants would find themselves in a new world of labour. Peasant farmers and craftsmen in the old country, they had laboured to provide for their families and to fulfill feudal obligations.

34

They had greater control of their time and activities, working in the fields with family members or in small craftsmaking shops. Traditions and ancient rules and understanding defined and regulated their work. But once in the islands, all of them would be thrust into a wage earning system and the regimented life of modern agricultural labour.[1]

The plantation work day began at 5 a.m. when the men gathered to wait for a truck or train ride to the fields. Except for a one-hour lunch break and a couple of brief rest periods, they worked until 4 p.m. They planted, weeded, fertilized, irrigated or harvested the sugar cane 10 hours a day, 26 days a month.

Plantation society was segregated along racial or ethnic lines. 'Haoles' (Caucasian Americans) were the managers; Portuguese and Spaniards were the overseers; Japanese were given the technical and mechanical jobs. Even when Japanese or Portuguese did the same work, they generally received more pay than Filipinos.

From 80 to 90% of field labour was done on the basis of the 'piece work' system in which the wages of a worker were determined not by the number of hours he worked, but by the amount of work he did. Field labourers were paid by the acre, by the ton, by the yard, or by the foot cultivated (...) About 5% earned the minimum one dollar a day (...) The able-bodied received at least sixty dollars monthly as cane loaders, fifty as portable track men or cane haulers, seventy-five as seed or cane netters, or sixty as watchmen.[2]

Because the majority of the Filipinos who came to Hawaii were men, it was difficult to develop a stable social life.

Although the HSPA voiced desires to bring wives and children along with the men, actual plantation policies discouraged this. First, the cost of living for a family on plantation wages made normal family life almost prohibitive. Secondly, plantation managers frowned on having to provide special housing, schooling, and medical aid to non-productive dependents. Early nurses on plantations even reported cases of forced sterilizations for women who were having too many children.[3]

In 1910 the ratio between Filipino men and women was ten to one, by 1930 five to one. This situation created problems peculiar to Hawaii Filipinos.

My mama said, If we live in that Filipino camp, too much trouble. Because, you know, that time in 1910 until 1917, '18, all those trouble in there, you know, not enough women, not enough women. So, whenever a newcomer from the island immigration, and then those old people in the camp in Hawaii, they meet all those newcomers. They see, trying to see, if there is a woman coming (...) they go make trouble to the newcomer because they want to take the women. We call that 'cowboy-cowboy'.[4]

The Depression years made it even more difficult for Hawaii Filipinos to develop a stable community life. The HSPA drastically cut back recruitment. After 1934, immigration to the US as a whole was limited to only 50 a year. Because few Filipinos were born in Hawaii and many were returning to the Philippines, the number of Filipinos in Hawaii declined. It was not until 1946, after the end of World War II, that another large group of Filipinos was allowed into Hawaii.

The postwar years

The Filipinos who came to Hawaii in 1946 were recruited in an attempt to break an industry-wide strike in the sugar plantations. After 1946, the immigration gates to Hawaii closed once again. By 1950, when there were 61,052, there were still 2,000 fewer Filipinos in Hawaii than there had been in 1930. With thousands of 'oldtimers' returning to the Philippines and immigration restricted, the percentage of Philippine-born among Hawaii Filipinos declined and the male to female ratio improved significantly, so that by 1960 there were only 1.8 men to every woman and the imbalance had almost disappeared among the younger age groups.[5]

These changes meant that the Filipino community in Hawaii became increasingly family-centred, rather than dominated by single males. This, in turn, meant that Filipinos began gradually to see themselves as Americans, or at least Hawaiians, rather than transient workers.

One of the indications of this community spirit was the founding of Filipino associations in various plantation towns and urban areas of Oahu. Filipinos began to expand their relationships with other Filipinos in the locality, rather than just with Filipinos coming from the same Filipino hometown. The United Filipino Council of Hawaii was founded in 1946, mainly as an attempt to get together and coordinate the activities of various associations on Oahu. In 1951, the various Filipino Catholic clubs in different localities decided to get together and hold their first territorial convention; they continued to hold one every year. The Filipino Chamber of Commerce was formed in 1954. In 1959, various Filipino community associations held their first territorial state convention.[6]

Changes in Filipino social life were linked to changes in the plantation system. Under pressure from an increasingly powerful union movement, plantation wages and working conditions improved significantly after World War II. Plantation towns also became less heavily regimented and paternalistic.

At the same time, increased mechanisation reduced employment in the rural areas and many Filipinos moved to the towns. In 1930 only 4,776 of the 63,052 Filipinos in Hawaii lived in Honolulu but by 1960 nearly one third had moved there. Indeed, some parts of Honolulu, especially the Halihi-Palama area, became predominantly Filipino.

Though Hawaii Filipinos now had a wider range of jobs to choose from,

WELCOME TO "MEET THE PRESS"!

OUR GUEST TODAY IS PRESIDENT CORAZON AQUINO!

MRS. AQUINO, WHAT IS YOUR ANALYSIS OF WHAT'S WRONG WITH THE PHILIPPINE ECONOMY?

IT'S IN HAWAII!

BILL SANDERS/MILWAKE JOURNAL

movement from low-status, low-pay occupations towards jobs with better pay and higher status was slow. In 1960 half of the Hawaii Filipino population were employed as 'labourers, service and household workers' compared to only 23% of the whole Hawaiian population. Another 22% of Filipino workers were 'equipment operators'. Only 3% were 'managers, officials and proprietors' compared to 12% for the total population.[7]

The liberalisation of immigration laws in 1965 brought a new wave of Filipinos to Hawaii. Filipinos accounted for more than half of the immigrants to Hawaii in the period from 1965 to 1974, averaging close to 4,000 per year.

Since most of these immigrants were relatives of Hawaii Filipinos, they were generally more rural in origin and had less schooling than those immigrants who went to the mainland. The movement to Honolulu, entry into non-plantation employment and other demographic trends noted in the 1960s continued into the 1970s. In the late 1970s the Hawaii Filipino community was concentrated at both ends of the age spectrum — young Honolulu Filipinos and ageing plantation workers.

The decline of the Hawaii sugar industry in the mid-1970s, coupled with the advanced age of most plantation Filipinos, made for pitifully poor

37

conditions. The growth of tourist industries did not prevent Hawaii from having the highest unemployment combined with the highest cost-of-living of all states of the US.

The position of Filipinos on some of the lowest rungs of Hawaii's occupational and income ladder (native Hawaiians were lower) meant that they suffered particularly from any downturn in Hawaii's economy. In 1970, more than a third of Hawaii Filipinos from plantation towns were living below the poverty line.

California dreaming

Until 1960 California Filipinos were the second largest group of Filipinos in the US after Hawaii. California Filipinos were similarly affected by broad trends in Filipino immigration to the US: the heavy influx of agricultural labourers after the exclusion of Chinese and Japanese in 1924 was followed by the exclusion of Filipinos after the passage of the Tydings-McDuffie Act in 1934. Many war brides and families entered after changes in legal restrictions were introduced following World War II. Finally, there was a new immigration inflow after 1965.

The contrasting political economy of the two states, however, caused the two communities to develop quite differently. In contrast to the relatively stable work cycle in Hawaii's sugar plantations, California's reliance on fruit and vegetable products created a seasonal demand for labour. Filipino agricultural workers therefore followed the planting and harvesting schedule. California's larger industrial base, especially after World War II, as well as its large and diverse urban centres, also created employment opportunities. For this reason, California has attracted a large number of Filipino immigrants in recent years.

Large-scale Filipino immigration to California started a full decade later than it did in Hawaii. In 1920 there were still only 2,674 Filipinos in California, about half of whom were labourers who had left the Hawaii plantations. The rest were either *pensionados* (sent to the US by the American colonial government to train for clerical and public school teaching positions in the Philippines) or houseboys brought into the country by army officers returning from a tour of duty in the Philippines.[8]

Over the next 10 years numbers grew rapidly. By 1930, 30,000 Filipinos were living in the state, and growing numbers were being recruited directly from the Philippines. About 40% of California's entire agricultural labour force at this time were Filipino.

Filipino farm workers were organised into work teams by Japanese, Caucasian and (by the 1930s) Filipino contractors. Workers would be taken to the fields in buses, live in a migrant camp for one or two weeks, then move to another camp.

In February to March the Filipino was to be found south, in El Centro, California, packing winter vegetables and melons, helping in farm or poultry work, or pruning and spraying fruit trees. From April to August, he was in Delano, Fresno, Salinas, Stockton or even further north in the

Marcelo and Ana

Marcelo was a colonel in the Philippine Army. He graduated near the top of his class in the Philippine Military Academy and later finished a masters degree in management from a top Manila school. He was always promoted ahead of his classmates. But because he is not part of the ruling clique in Marcos' military, he remained at the rank of colonel.

Marcelo's wife Ana is the daughter of a Filipino in the US Navy. She is an American citizen, but she wanted to live in the Philippines with her husband and raise her children there. In June 1982, she came to the United States alone, hoping to earn enough money as a nurse to send her three grown children to college. Marcelo stayed, refusing to believe that a career which had spanned 25 years of his life was over.

In 1985, Marcelo finally came to the United States to join his wife and their three younger children. He spent six months looking for a job. The only one he found was as a security guard. But he could not accept the fact that his supervisor was a retired sergeant in the US Army. His wife was already working two shifts and they still did not have enough.

Marcelo is desperate but he cannot swallow his pride and work as a security guard. Instead, he has pinned his hopes on joining an insurance and investment savings firm. Selling insurance and real estate is a typical job for college-educated Filipinos with no marketable technical skills. It provides at least an illusion of security for a Filipino community made anxious by low-paying jobs, discrimination, and being 11,000 miles away from home.

Marcelo and Ana are better educated and better equipped to stabilize their family situation than most Filipinos in the United States. But their experience exemplifies the condition of the Filipino community in the United States today — the economic and political 'push' factors behind their departure, the difficulties of finding jobs and financial security, the family connections and the established Filipino community that cushions the difficulties of getting settled in a foreign land.

Salinas valley picking hops, or he was in the apple orchards off Washington, or in the fishing canneries of Alaska. In September, he returned to the cities and waited for the following year's cycle, surviving only on the little he had saved from migrant labour until he could start earning again in February or March.[9]

The work was hard, life in the camps and on the road gruelling.

We travelled. I mean, we moved from camp to camp (...) My mother cooked and my stepfather ran out in the fields and worked from four o'clock in the morning until they finished, usually around one o'clock. I remember them going out with flashlights on their heads just like miners so they could get to the asparagus before it grew (…) From the asparagus season, we would migrate to Fairfield, to Suison and there the men worked out in the orchards picking fruits while the women and even children, as long as they could stand on their boxes, were cutting fruits.[10]

Earnings were as meagre as the work was hard. Manuel Buaken, a field hand who, with Carlos Bulosan, was an eloquent chronicler of the Filipino experience in California, recalled that in 1927 he earned $2.50 a day for a ten-hour day, six days-a-week work cycle. Nationally, the average pay for farm workers was $2.28 a day while factory workers earned $5.52.[11] Because Filipino farm workers were generally single males who moved constantly from camp to camp and did not develop stable family or community ties, they were often prey to corrupt contractors, gamblers, and prostitutes. The pool hall and the taxi dance hall were the characteristic gathering places of Filipinos when they were not at work.

Racial discrimination

Prior to 1946 Filipinos in California were legally barred from voting, owning property or marrying Caucasian women. Ironically, part of the legal justification for anti-Filipino discrimination was that Filipinos were 'wards' of the American colonial government and therefore were neither aliens nor citizens. The fact that Filipinos have never constituted more than 4% of California's total population and do not have much political clout may partly explain why anti-Filipino racism has been more virulent in California than in Hawaii, where they represent a significant segment of the population.

Racist legal restrictions combined with depressed economic conditions to create a vicious circle. Because Filipinos earned very little, they often lived in overcrowded apartments and rooming houses. This contributed to the anti-Filipino stereotype of unkempt, unsanitary people willing to 'live like pigs'. When Filipinos managed to save enough money to buy family homes, however, they were barred from doing so. Anti-Filipino racism reached its height during the period of the Great Depression in the early 1930s. Economic hard times led to increased economic and social discrimination, physical harassment and, in a number of instances, vigilante action. In October 1929, for example, 300 whites from Exeter in California invaded a Filipino farm labour camp and burned a barn after a Filipino stabbed a white man at a carnival. In January 1930, a mob of 500 men went on the rampage in Watsonville, burning Filipino homes and buildings, killing two and beating scores of Filipinos.

Unsatisfied with vigilante action, Californian racists moved to bar Filipino immigration and drive out those already in the country. The Tydings-McDuffie provision limiting Filipino immigration to 50 per year was put in at the behest of Californian politicians, and the following year the same

> In a letter dated May 5 1908, the vice president of H. Hackfeld and Company confirmed the purchase order of supplies for George Wilcox of Grove Farm Plantation. Appearing after 'fertiliser' in the alphabetical list was the item 'Filipinos'.
> Ron Takaki, *Pah Hana: Plantation Life and Labour in Hawaii.*

politicians put together a repatriation plan. But less than 2,500 took up the offer.

For many of its victims, anti-Filipino racism was doubly galling because it went so radically against the image of an egalitarian America that had drawn them to emigrate. This was the theme of much of the writing of the period — of Carlos Bulosan's *America In The Heart*, for example.

It was the same persistent dream of fraternity that led many Filipinos to enlist in the US armed forces after Pearl Harbor and the invasion of the Philippines in 1941. Ironically, the first batch of Filipino volunteers was turned away: being neither aliens nor citizens, they could not join. It was not until several months later that the requirements of the American war effort and the romance of the defence of Bataan and Corregidor combined to make Filipino enlistment possible. In all, more than 7,000 Filipinos joined the American armed forces, almost all of them in the First Filipino Infantry Division.

War brides

World War II ushered in a period of rapid change for US Filipinos. In 1942 the US Congress passed a resolution allowing Filipinos to become naturalised citizens. In the same year, laws prohibiting the employment of Filipinos in government jobs were lifted. Starting in 1945 Filipinos were allowed to own land in California. Anti-miscegenation laws were repealed in 1948.

Although the Philippine immigration quota was raised to only 100 per year after independence in 1946, thousands of long-time residents acquired citizenship and were able to bring relatives to the US. The total number of Filipinos in the US declined from 108,260 in 1930 to 98,132 in 1940; but by 1950 the total had jumped to 122,698. Apart from the 7,500 recruited by Hawaii sugar planters in 1946, the bulk of the new immigrants were 'war brides' — wives of Filipino American servicemen.

'War bride' immigration had a tremendous impact on the Filipino community. In California, for example, the number of female Filipinos listed by the census jumped from 1,500 in 1940 to more than 5,000 in 1950. In 1940 only 5,327 out of 26,313 Filipino males in the state were married. By 1950 the number had risen to 17,616. With the exception of the oldest Filipino men, the community changed rapidly from one dominated by single men to a stable, family-centred community.

For the most part, the second wave 'war brides' did not face the same

41

degree of economic instability previously experienced by their husbands or other members of the first wave. At least, for those who stayed connected to the military, certain essential needs were provided such as government housing and medical care. Even for those who left the armed services, special veterans' loans helped people buy homes and automobiles. And most important of all, the returning GI's were granted full citizenship. Citizenship opened doors to civil service positions.[12]

Discrimination against Filipinos was nowhere more evident than in the US Navy, where most of the Filipinos in the US armed forces were concentrated. As early as 1919, there were already some 6,000 Filipinos in the US Navy, and between 1944 and 1973 about 22,000 were recruited under an arrangement worked out after independence. Since many of these men remained in the navy for much of their working lives, the number remained high. Including Filipino Americans, 16,669 were listed in 1970.

Though a range of jobs became available to Filipino servicemen from the 1960s, it remained true even in 1970 that 80% of the Filipinos in the Navy were stewards — a rank which has the lowest status and pay in the service. More than 80% of all stewards (9,000 of 11,000) were Filipinos. In addition to being unable to get promotion, Filipinos often had to deal with officers who treated them as servants.

Yeah, they called you boy. That was a common expression with Americans. Some of us were adults and resented name-calling and stuff like that, but in the military you cannot object everytime you hear the word or else the relation between you and your superior officer will start to get more delicate.[13]

Resistance

There have been plenty of reasons for Filipino resistance throughout the seventy or so years of the community's existence in the US. For many Filipinos, surviving severe racial discrimination and abominable economic conditions is victory enough. What others see as quiet, stoic acceptance is often the opposite of what it seems. As one Filipino sailor explained:

The officers, some of them from the South, were really very nasty, they thought you were a servant through an act of Congress, that you were inducted to be their personal servant. Well, some of them learned the hard way. They didn't know what was going on in the kitchen. Yeah, that's right, they didn't know how their coffee was made — with our socks that we had worn for a week. And that some of their food had Filipino saliva in it. Sometimes it took a while until someone told them that the worst enemy you could have was your steward.[14]

Resistance was not limited to individual acts. Filipinos were in the forefront of union organising in both Hawaii and California. In Hawaii, the Filipino Federation of Labor (FFL) was formed in 1919 under the leadership of

The United States

> When a Caucasian woman filed an assault case against her Filipino lover in 1936, San Francisco municipal court judge Sylvain Lazarus wrote a decision in which, among other things, he said: 'This is a deplorable situation (...). It is a dreadful thing when these Filipinos, scarcely more than savages, come to San Francisco, work for practically nothing, and obtain the society of these girls. Because they work for nothing, decent white boys cannot get jobs.'
> H. Brett Melendy, 'California Discrimination Against Filipinos, 1927-1935'.

Pablo Manlapit, a plantation worker. The following year, the FFL joined with Japanese unions to form the Higher Wage Movement. It was this movement that spearheaded industry-wide strikes in 1920 and 1924.

Both strikes were defeated through the use of a wide range of often brutal tactics. During the strike in 1924, for example, 16 workers were killed by police in one incident alone. The Hawaii Sugar Planters Association also 'imported' large numbers of Filipinos to work as scabs. Filipino labour leaders including Manlapit were harassed, jailed and/or forcibly expelled from the islands.

Although an 85-day strike of Filipino plantation workers in 1936 won recognition for the union and a small pay increase, it was not until after World War II that plantation workers succeeded in developing a union strong enough to secure significant improvements in plantation pay and working conditions. By working closely with middle class Japanese politicians in the Democratic Party, the International Longshoremen's and Warehousemen's Union (ILWU) combined political clout with successful multi-ethnic organising among plantation workers.[15]

In California, the powerful Associated Farmers of California successfully staved off unionisation of farm workers until the late 1960s. Organising among Filipino farm workers reached its peak during the Depression years. In 1934, the Filipino Labor Union (FLU) had seven branch offices in the state and some 2,000 active members. In 1934, the FLU organised a strike in the lettuce fields of Salinas, California.

This strike was broken easily due to vigilante mobs, pressure from merchants, and a double standard of law enforcement designed to thwart Filipino labour unity. While the Salinas strike was only one of more than 20 Filipino labour disputes between 1930 and 1936, it was a seminal turning point in the evolution of Filipino labour unions. The strike resulted in organised labour militancy on the part of Filipino farm workers, thus destroying the prevalent stereotype of happy Filipino labourers who worked willingly for low wages.[16]

Anti-communism was one of the most important weapons California planters used to stop Filipinos from organising themselves. In 1949, for example, the US Justice Department ordered the arrest of leaders of the

43

Alaska Cannery Workers Union. The Justice Department accused them of being communist and ordered their deportation. [17]

The struggle of farm workers in California during the 1960s and 1970s was led primarily by the Chicano United Farm Workers. Nevertheless the first contract with a large California grower was won by the largely Filipino Agricultural Workers Organising Committee (AWOC), led by Larry Itliong, after a grape pickers strike in 1965. AWOC later merged with the National Farm Workers Association led by Cesar Chavez to form the United Farm Workers. [18]

Today: Between two worlds

Today there are at least one million Filipinos living legally in the US. Perhaps half a million more, according to some estimates, are living illegally, as *Tago Nang Tago* (TNTs). Numbers have grown very sharply in the last few decades, primarily because of direct immigration (35,000 per year) and the high birthrate within the community. The 1980 census listed 774,640 Filipinos, compared with 98,000 in 1940 and 176,000 in 1960. [19]

According to the census, more than two-thirds of US Filipinos were living on the West Coast in 1950: nearly 500,000 lived in the two states of California and Hawaii alone. The next largest concentrations of Filipinos were in Illinois (43,839), New York (33,956), New Jersey (24,377) and Virginia (18,901). Most were concentrated in large urban centres, such as Chicago and New York, a pattern of distribution which has probably not changed much in the last five years, except in Texas, where the rapid growth of the Filipino population in cities such as Houston and Dallas has probably more than tripled the 15,096 Filipinos listed in the state in 1980.

This distribution is the result of various factors including weather, job availability, and the existence of established Filipino communities. Jobs are no more plentiful in California and Hawaii than in other states, but the warm weather and the presence of established Filipino communities have been a powerful magnet.

Family and friends are the main sources of assistance and information about housing, jobs, and schools for newly arrived immigrants. About 15,000 of the 35,000 Filipinos who enter the United States annually as immigrants receive their visas because they are relatives of Filipinos with American citizenship. Apart from support provided by family and friends, the existence of established Filipino communities also means Filipino grocery stores, restaurants, video and audio tape stores, community newspapers and radio programmes.

For doctors, nurses and other professionals, state licensing requirements have been a major factor determining residence. California, for example, has difficult licensing requirements, and doctors and nurses have therefore tended to gravitate towards cities like Chicago and New York. The booming sunbelt economy of Texas and the warm, hospitable weather of cities such as Houston and Dallas are the main reasons behind the rapid growth of the Filipino communities there.

The relatively wider range of job opportunities available to the

professionals and other college-educated Filipinos who have formed a large proportion of post-1965 immigrants has been the key factor behind the rapid growth of Filipino communities in states outside Hawaii and California. In the past, concentrations of Filipinos were determined largely by available jobs in agriculture (Hawaii and California), the fish canning industry (Seattle, Washington) and the existence of naval bases (San Diego and Alameda in California and Norfolk, Virginia).

Occupational degradation

Though national tabulations from the 1980 census for the Filipino community have not yet been released, figures compiled by Professor Amado Cebezas from the University of California at Berkeley, using 1980 census figures for California, Hawaii, Illinois and New York, provide a good picture of the occupational and income status of U.S. Filipinos. Filipinos in those four states account for 72% of U.S. Filipinos. Earlier census data and a variety of surveys can be used to fill in grey areas in the total picture.

All these sources indicate that, relative both to the majority Caucasian population and to other minority groups, Filipinos are disproportionately represented in manual labour jobs or in low-skilled, low-income occupations in the service industries. These sources also show that, whereas before World War II Filipinos were predominantly farm workers, by the 1980s they were represented across the full range of occupations. There are also distinct differences between Filipino communities in Hawaii, California, and the mid-Western and Eastern states.

In Hawaii and California, where more than half of the US Filipinos reside, the majority work in low-status, low-income jobs classified as 'sales/clerical', 'food/cleaning service workers', and 'operators, fabricators, labourers'. In Hawaii, 34.5% of employed Filipinos work as chambermaids, bellboys and waiters in the tourist industry. In California, only 13.4% are in similar jobs, but 38.9% are in sales and clerical jobs. A good many Filipinos are also 'operators, fabricators and labourers' — 22.1% in Hawaii and 15.4% in California. By 1980, only 2.1% of California Filipinos remained

45

farm labourers, though 11.2% of those in Hawaii still fell into this category. California counted more Filipino 'managers and professionals' (19.7%) than Hawaii (5.5%), but far fewer than Illinois (38.9%) and New York (43.8%). A larger proportion of Filipinos in Illinois and New York had managerial or professional jobs than the general population (22.7% in Illinois, 26.3% in New York). Another large category of Eastern US Filipino jobs is 'sales/clerical' (35.1% in Illinois; 38.7% in New York).

Overall, there has been a clear shift from manual labour towards the service industries, which reflects a general shift in the American economy.

The proportion of Filipino immigrants with professional and technical skills has also risen, from one to three in ten between 1965 and 1970. In some areas, there has been a striking change. Between 1962 and 1965, for example, 182 Filipino engineers migrated to the US; over a similar four-year period between 1967 and 1970, 3,323 did so. During the same period, the number of medical immigrants (doctors, nurses, dentists and medical technicians) jumped from 837 to 8,477.[20]

These changes have not led, however, to a corresponding improvement in status and income. One reason for this is that, as service industries have absorbed an even larger proportion of the American labour force, wage levels within these occupations have plummeted relative to other occupations.[21] Another reason is that Filipinos suffer from serious occupational discrimination. A 1977 study of the salaries in California, for example, showed that more than half the Filipinos with professional qualifications were working as clerical, sales and wage labourers.[22] And the California Health and Welfare Agency published a report in 1982 which showed that:

● Filipinos earned less than the majority of Americans of the same educational level;
● The number of Filipinos with high school or college degrees who were overqualified for their jobs was far higher than the national average;
● Although there were twice as many college-educated Filipino women compared to the rest of the population, they earned only half the wages of their counterparts.[23]

Statistics have helped conceal the enormous problem. The mean family income of New York Filipinos in 1980 was US$27,955, for example, compared to US$24,168 for the total population. In Illinois, the gap was even wider in favour of Filipino families ($34,384 to $25,980). These family incomes, however, hide the lower incomes of individual workers. Illinois Filipino families had 2.3 working members compared to only 1.6 for the total population. New York figures were roughly the same: 2.1 workers per family among Filipinos compared to 1.5 for the total population. But in Hawaii and California, Filipino families had lower incomes despite the fact that they had more family members working.

It is usual for both husband and wife to work, often at two full-time jobs each. After high school, the children are also encouraged to work. Expenses

SORIN MASCA

are kept low because everyone lives together. With parents working more than one job and two or three children working, the family income can be sufficient to pay house mortgages and payments on cars and home appliances. The material conditions for middle class consciousness are thus acquired even if the jobs mean occupational downgrading and endless drudgery.

The low-skill, low-income jobs of most US Filipinos certainly cannot be explained by lack of education or training. The average length of education of US Filipinos in 1970 was 12.2 years, longer than that of the US population as a whole. The 1980 census figures are even more stark. In New York, 68% of Filipinos had four or more years of college education compared to 19% for the total population; in Illinois, it was 67% to 16%; in California, 44% to 20%. Only in Hawaii did a smaller proportion of the Filipino community (20%) have college level education than the general population (22%).

Class expectations

Despite these conditions, enough Filipinos succeed in establishing themselves as professionals to sustain the dreams of those who fail. This, and

'It is true that we are American citizens now, but are we given the same rights and privileges as other American citizens? If we are good enough to be shot at in time of war, we should be good enough to enjoy all the rights of a free man.' A Filipino-American adjutant, 1946.
Edwin Almiral, *Ethnic Identity and Social Negotiation: A Study of a Filipino Community in California.*

the shame of failure, prevent all but a handful from returning home. And though the vast majority of Filipinos work out their hopes in the dreary confines of the lower rungs of the US working class, many retain their middle class aspirations, helped by the yawning gulf in living standards between the two countries. In the Philippines, only upper class Filipinos earn enough to own homes and cars, while in the US, working class people can also acquire these hallmarks of American living.

Racism

It is difficult to disparage the Filipino community's hard work, ingenuity and persistence. What Filipinos have achieved despite widespread racism and discrimination should not be belittled.

Racial and national discrimination has been particularly hard on the one third of the community born in the US. As children, it is easy to feel that you are no different from the next kid, especially in ethnically diverse states such as California and Hawaii. It is all the harder then to accept, or emotionally comprehend, discrimination in later years. And it is easy to understand why the characteristic Filipino response to the political ferment of the 1960s was the 'Filipino identity movement'.

The more progressive elements in this movement were in the forefront of anti-discrimination struggles during the 1970s. Together with other Third World students, they fought for affirmative action programmes and ethnic studies courses in academic departments. They fought to extend the benefits of the Afro-American civil rights movement to Asian-American communities. They worked with organisations of Filipino professionals for fair licensing procedures.

Much was achieved in all these areas of struggle. But mounting frustrations later gave way to a realisation that it would be extremely difficult to develop stable organisations, with significant influence in the community, capable of sustaining the anti-discrimination struggle from one issue to another. Powerful nationwide campaigns, mobilising at times thousands of Filipinos, left little in the way of organisational structures to prepare for future campaigns.

With the exception of ILWU branches in Hawaii and Seattle, Filipinos abandoned the labour unions which had been their most important instruments of struggle between 1930 and the 1950s. The geographical and occupational dispersal of Filipinos has made it difficult to organise Filipino unions. Professional organisations of doctors, nurses, or accountants seldom grew beyond state boundaries. Even the Union of Democratic

Filipinos, one of the few well organised, nationwide Filipino American organisations, went into a period of decline in the early 1980s.

One of the reasons why it is so difficult to mobilise Filipino Americans into political organisations is their preoccupation with 'making it' in a different economic situation. It is hard to find time to attend meetings when you hold down two eight hour jobs. When Filipinos do join community organisations, more often than not they will be 'hometown organisations' — the 'Boholano Circles' and 'Filam Ilongos' that dot the Filipino community landscape.

Politics

Until February 1986 the dominant political issue in the US Filipino community was the Marcos dictatorship and US government support for it. In the post-Marcos era the political life of the US Filipino community continues to mirror in important ways the political life of the Philippines. To be sure, there are many Filipino Americans, especially those born in the United States, who see themselves as primarily part of the American political system, but the only organisations which are nationwide in scope and have persisted over a period of years are those anchored on support for popular struggles in the Philippines.

President Aquino and her late husband spent three years (1980-83) in exile in the United States. After Benigno 'Ninoy' Aquino was murdered, many wealthy anti-Marcos Filipinos sought safety in the United States, and these former exiles now perform important functions for the Aquino government. One of the most important is to ensure continued US support for the Aquino administration.

For a significant section of those who remained in the United States, their work centres on opposing continued US intervention in the Philippines. While supporting humanitarian assistance, groups such as the Alliance for Philippine Concerns believe that American dominance in Philippines economic and political life is an important cause of poverty and underdevelopment. They also feel that the continuing crisis of the Philippines bears heavily on the condition of US Filipinos. A Philippines which has undergone a genuine transformation of its social and economic structures will be a place where Filipinos will stay and work in confidence that they can secure better lives for themselves and their families. It will also persuade many of those living in the United States that they still have a home they can return to and work for.

5. CANADA

'Newly-arrived Filipino immigrants face two particular problems when they seek work in Canada. They are required to have 'Canadian experience' and their educational and professional qualifications in the Philippines are not recognised in Canada.'

Filipino immigrants are beginning to form a distinct population group within Canada's multi-racial society. Estimates by the Philippine Ministry of Labor and by the Canadian Embassy in Manila suggest that there are more than 100,000 Filipino-Canadians spread throughout the country.

The first Filipinos came to Canada after World War II. About 5,000 arrived between 1956 and 1966 and during this period the government's immigration statistics lumped Filipinos in the category of nationals from 'countries not British'.

At this time it was very difficult, in fact, for Filipinos and other non-Caucasians to enter Canada, because the government maintained a colour bar. Only after 1962, when racial discrimination was formally expunged from the statute book, and as the growing demand for skilled labour encouraged more flexible immigration policies, did it become much easier for skilled migrants to enter the country and for relatives of settled immigrants to join their families.

In some instances, Filipinos were offered incentives to take jobs in Canada — in Ontario, for example, nurses were given free hotel accommodation and other fringe benefits — and from the end of the 1960s the number of Filipinos entering Canada began to increase sharply. According to official figures, by 1971 there were more than 20,000 Filipino-Canadians. A significant number also entered the country illegally. In 1972 these people were offered an amnesty and given the opportunity to acquire landed immigrant status.

1972 was also the year in which President Marcos declared Martial Law. This caused immigration to rise sharply again — from 4,000 in 1972 to 6,500 in 1973 and 9,500 in 1974. During the nine years of Martial Law an average of nearly 7,000 Filipinos emigrated to Canada each year.

After 1977, when a new immigration act was introduced, it again became rather more difficult for Filipinos to enter Canada. Until 1977, foreign nationals had been barred from entering Canada if they worked to topple democratic governments. A bill introduced that year (Bill C-24) widened the scope of this clause and refused right of entry to people who sought the overthrow of *any* government. This clause, which is difficult to justify on political or philosophical grounds, clearly discriminated against refugees.

Distribution of Filipinos in Canada

There are pockets of Filipino-Canadians in practically every major province in Canada. The largest community is found in Ontario, where 29,175 Filipinos were officially registered in 1979 — and where up to 40,000 live today. The populations of Manitoba and British Columbia, which each had 9,000 in 1979, have probably doubled since, and more than 4,500 live in

Alberta and in Quebec. The latter's reputation as a 'beautiful city' attracted many Filipinos, but the Quebec Language Law has hindered many from settling, even though the province offers subsidised French language courses.

There are also smaller communities in Saskatchewan, Nova Scotia, New Brunswick, Prince Edward Island and Newfoundland. A small group of Filipinos even live in the Yukon in the remote North Western Territory.

In various parts of Canada some urban areas are acquiring 'Filipino character' — Winnipeg has a street called 'Manila', and wherever there are groups of Filipinos, Filipino-owned businesses have sprung up — food stores, travel agencies and beauty salons.

Work skills

Until about 1972, most of the Filipinos coming to Canada were attracted by the economic opportunities, rather than 'pushed out' by conditions inside the Philippines. Most of the immigrants during this period were skilled or professional workers — assets to Canada but a 'brain drain' from the Philippines.

Professionals made up more than half (53%) of arrivals, and secretarial and clerical workers another 25%, while less than 10% were manufacturing and assembly line workers.

There was also a highly unbalanced sex ratio. During the second half of the 1960s, two thirds of new immigrants were women, who took up jobs as nurses, medical technologists, secretaries and clerks.

After Martial Law was declared, this situation changed. Emigrants remember the long queue of Filipinos lining up at the Canadian Embassy as many more Filipinos began to emigrate to escape domestic political and economic problems.

Between 1967 and 1975 there was a considerable increase in the number of arriving Filipinos who were over 40 years of age. This was particularly true of the women. Whereas only 1,209 (19%) of immigrants in 1969 and 1970 were over 35, in 1980 and 1981 4,506 (38%) of the 11,897 Filipinos who arrived in Canada were over 40 years old.

There was an equally clear increase in the number of very young children. The number of Filipino children under nine years old doubled between 1971 and 1975, when they represented 42% of the arrivals.

As a direct result, a much lower proportion of new arrivals since the 1970s have been economically active. In 1967, 88% intended to take the nearest job behind a desk or in a factory but in 1975 more than 50% of Filipino immigrants were not available for employment.

Since then, the trend has continued, and of the 11,897 Filipinos who migrated to Canada in 1980-81, 7,729 (64%) recorded themselves as dependents — spouses, children and relatives. In a Canadian labour market in which jobs were no longer easy to come by, this has meant fewer people joining the unemployment queues.

The old Filipino-Canadian stereotypes of nurses in starched white uniforms, medical technologists or efficient secretaries typing 75 words per minute are also becoming out of date. Many Filipino-Canadians are now active in the manufacturing and service sectors. Of the 2,317 workers admitted to Canada in 1981, 864 (37%) had industrial skills. Until most of them were laid off in 1981-82, about 500 Filipino-Canadians worked at the Crown Corporation De Havilland Aircraft factory in Downsview, Ontario. In Vancouver, many work in the publicly owned telephone, insurance and hydro-electrical corporations.

More than 20% of those employed in Winnipeg's garment industry are Filipino-Canadians. Many were recruited directly from the Philippines because they were experienced operators of industrial sewing machines. Wages in the garment and textile industry, where the workers are mainly women, are among the lowest in Canada, and workers in the industry are not well organised. Filipino women had the reputation of being particularly passive until they took part in an important strike at the TAN-JAY Company in 1982. Because most of the textile workers lack higher education, and have a working-class background, they are often looked down on by other members of the Filipino-Canadian community and even edged out of Filipino social and cultural organisations.

Many Filipino women have found employment as domestic workers. Unlike the majority of Filipinos, domestics are not considered to be immigrants but rather contractual workers on temporary visas. According to the Ad Hoc Committee of Filipino Domestic Workers for Landed Status, 3,000 of the 11,000 foreign domestics in Canada in 1981 were Filipinos. Some of the domestics have come directly from the Philippines, but many have already worked in Hong Kong, European countries, or Singapore. As a rule, housemaids are well-educated and have worked in the Philippines as secretaries, teachers or clerks. More than any other group, they demonstrate how much the economic crisis in the Philippines has forced skilled workers to seek any job abroad, in order to support their families.

Discrimination

Newly-arrived Filipino immigrants face two particular problems when they seek work in Canada. They are required to have 'Canadian experience' and their educational and professional qualifications in the Philippines are not recognised in Canada.

Canadian professional associations — which control licensing of their professions — do not allow Filipinos, or immigrants from other Third World countries, to affiliate on the strength of qualifications they have acquired in their countries of origin. As a result many Filipino engineers have been reclassified as technicians, and professionals have had to take employment in unrelated fields or swallow their pride and take assembly line jobs. At the same time, other Filipinos have been driven to manual labour or the lowest-paying jobs because it is claimed they are 'over qualified' for ordinary office positions.

Many students also find it glaringly unjust that their Philippine educational background is not recognised. In general they are downgraded when they enrol in Canadian schools or universities, on the grounds that elementary education lasts for six years and high school for four years in the Philippines, whereas in Canada there are eight years of elementary schooling and four years of high school.

Racism is also a problem. In 1972, 24% complained that they were discriminated against in their job-hunting. Another 7% said they had experienced discrimination in public places, while 4% had faced difficulty in finding a home. On the whole, though there is obvious racial discrimination in Canadian society, most Filipinos have not united to oppose it.

With time, more and more Filipinos are shedding their Filipino citizenship and taking the oath of allegiance to Canada. In 1972 2,657 Filipinos, in a rapidly growing community of 24,846, had become Canadian citizens, but by 1980 nearly two-thirds had done so. An amendment to the Canadian Citizenship Act of February 1, 1977 permitted immigrants to apply for Canadian citizenship after three instead of five years' residence, which partly explains this growth. But the oppressive relations between Filipino citizens and the Marcos government must also be remembered.

Cultural life and associations

The churches are an important focus for many Filipino-Canadians. The majority are Catholic but two other religious denominations, considered minority groups in the Philippines, are among the most cohesive Filipino congregations in Canada.

The Iglesia ni Kristo (INK or the Church of Christ), which has its roots in the Philippines, has begun spreading its gospel in North America. INK adherents have active congregations in Calgary (Alberta), Montreal and Ottawa. Another minority church group in the Philippines, the Baptists, has also grouped its members in Canada. In Toronto, the First Filipino Baptist Church was officially formed out of bible study groups. The Filipino Baptists

Filipino cultural group, Winnipeg

55

also have a very active group in Vancouver.

There are numerous social and recreational associations wherever Filipinos are concentrated. Indeed, there are as many groups as there are common or conflicting interests. In Toronto alone there were close to forty Filipino-Canadian organisations in 1982; thirty-one in Vancouver; thirteen in Winnipeg; fifteen in Montreal; eight in Alberta; and six in Saskatchewan. Most of these organisations are geared towards annual social functions such as dances or picnics. A good number are sports clubs, particularly for basketball and bowling. More recently, golf has also become popular — in the Philippines it is a rich sport, quite out of the reach of ordinary wage-earners. Senior citizens have formed their own circles, while a few organisations group Filipinos from particular regions — the Ilongo-speaking provinces in the Visayas or the Bicol region.

In Toronto, there are two well-established community centres where newly arrived immigrants can drop in for help with settlement problems. The Silayan Community Centre pioneered community service among Filipino-Canadians in the city. At present operating under the Catholic charities, it provides free space where Filipino-Canadian senior citizens can pass the time together singing, dancing or doing handicrafts. The Kababayan Community Service Centre, funded by Canadian government agencies, is more than just a welcoming centre for recently landed immigrants. It campaigned, for example, against the Ku Klux Klan, when it set up its headquarters in the same part of the city. It also helps Filipino domestics to find temporary work visas.

Many of these organisations are vocal about the need for 'unity'. Nevertheless, they remain fragmented. While they may unite to own or run a building — a Filipino-Canadian cultural centre in Toronto or Winnipeg, for example — more general unity has not been achieved and there is no national umbrella organisation representing Filipino-Canadians.

The United Council of Filipino Associations in Canada (UCFAC), founded in 1963 and subsidised by federal funds, aspired to play this role. But over its 15 years of life, it did little except organise a yearly 'junket' for elite community leaders. Dormant from 1977 to 1981, UCFAC received a frail new lease of life after a controversial convention in Winnipeg in 1982.

Its revival came at a time when groups in Toronto were attempting to build a 'national congress' of organisations — though, sadly, only in the Toronto area.

The social life of all these organisations is chronicled in the Filipino-Canadian press and media. In 1978 there were six Filipino-Canadian community newspapers in Toronto, as well as two radio programmes and a television show. Winnipeg had two publications, three television programmes and a radio programme. Montreal ran two monthly publications, and in Vancouver there was a television show. Unfortunately, many of these programmes and publications were short-lived and unprofessional. By the end of 1982, only *Balita* (a bi-monthly), *Atin Ito* (monthly), and *Filipiniana* (every two months) were still being produced, while in Winnipeg the monthly *Silangan* was floundering.

6. EUROPE

KITCHEN

'Look at me now, I'm old already and I still have to send £100 a month home to educate my nieces and nephews. How could I get married? ... I got the opportunity to come to Britain and it is my duty to help my family.'

A Filipina in London

BRITAIN

Filipino migrant workers started coming to Britain in large numbers during the early 1970s. Estimates vary as to how many are in Britain now. According to the *Department of Employment Gazette*, 20,226 work permits were issued to Filipinos between 1968 and 1980. But Filipinos have also come as students and visitors and taken work later, changing their status in the process; some have married Britons. In addition, Britain is one of the countries in which there is a relatively active 'Brides for Sale' trade.

There are perhaps 25,000 Filipinos living in the United Kingdom, about 85% of whom are women.[1] The great majority of Filipinos work in the health service and in the hotel and catering industries. About 90% of Filipinos in Britain have had at least two years' college training in the Philippines.[2] Many are qualified teachers, nurses, technicians, commerce graduates, secretaries, social workers, engineers and accountants. Almost all entered Britain under the 'work permit' system (see page 59), and the jobs they do make little or no use of their qualifications.

In 1979 about 47% of Filipinos in Britain were working in hospitals and welfare homes, as resident domestics, canteen workers, auxiliaries or state enrolled nurses.[3]

The next largest category are those working in the hotel and catering industry, where many married couples work as chambermaids and waiters. In 1976, 856 of the 2,050 Filipinos who entered this country went into private domestic service. Here again, most were women.[4]

Geographical distribution

Filipinos are scattered throughout the country. The largest communities are to be found in Aberdeen, Glasgow and Edinburgh in Scotland, and in Leeds, Manchester, Liverpool and Birmingham in England. But the majority now live in London and the surrounding counties. In recent years many Filipinos have chosen to move into London from other parts of the country in order to be closer to their friends and relatives, and it is not uncommon to find that Filipinos working in the same hospital or old people's home belong to the same village or barrio in the Philippines. For example, out of 33 Filipinos working in one old people's home in Hampstead, 28 come from the same village.

Practically all those living in London itself have at least one additional or part-time job. It is a common pattern for hospital staff to work from 6:30 am to 1 pm, do a second job in a hotel from 2.00-4.30 pm, then return to the hospital to work from 5 pm to 8 pm. Night duty hospital workers often have a

Europe

part-time job for two of their off days. Hotel workers may work through from 6 am to 3 pm, and do overtime between 5 pm and 8 pm, or from 8 pm to 11 pm. Many also take additional jobs, cleaning offices or private houses for two to three hours a day, two or three times a week. Almost all additional jobs involve unsocial hours, weekends, nights, or split duties.

How British immigration law affects Filipinos

Most Filipinos who came to Britain in the early to mid-1970s arrived under the 'work permit' scheme, which allowed foreign workers to take up a quota of semi-skilled jobs for resident domestics in private homes and hospitals, and chambermaids, cooks, waiters, and waitresses in hotels and restaurants. Work permits were issued by the Department of Employment to a specific employer for a named employee to do a specific job. They were only granted after employers had shown that they had unsuccessfully advertised the job concerned within Britain (over a period of six weeks), and were issued for periods of one year, renewed annually three times. After four years, a worker could apply to have restrictions lifted, could compete 'freely' for jobs and could settle in Britain.

Only childless couples and single women without dependent children were permitted to take work as resident domestics, and those applying for jobs in hotel and catering (and resident domestics from 1975) had to produce evidence of experience of similar work overseas.

The majority of Filipino workers who came to Britain were recruited through agencies in Britain or in the Philippines which organised the transaction through the payment of a fee from the employers. The workers who were recruited also paid large sums for processing their air tickets and papers. The sums involved (including a one-way air ticket) rose from £500-£600 in the early 1970s to over £1,000 by the end of the decade.

Most intended to repay the loans over a fairly short period, and then return to the Philippines. However, many agencies misrepresented the opportunities for saving in Britain, and on arrival Filipinos found themselves in low paid jobs from which they could not support their relatives in the Philippines while saving for their return. In some cases, there was outright fraud and job conditions bore little relation to the work they had been promised. In 1973, the Department of Employment temporarily banned work permits for semi-skilled or unskilled Filipinos after a charity revealed that a large group of Filipino women in a Rochdale textile factory were being paid £13 per week instead of the £40 they had been promised. In addition, they were living in insanitary and overcrowded accommodation — eight women to a room — and part of their wages was being stopped by their employers, the Alderglen Company, towards repayment of their airfares.[5]

Most Filipinos have been less dramatically exploited, but they are nonetheless locked into a cycle of debt. Helen came to Britain in 1973 to earn £12 per week as the resident domestic of a family. Though £4 was deducted from her wages to repay her air fare, she planned to save enough to set up a small business in the Philippines. More than a decade later Helen is still working in Britain, now sending £100 every month to support the large

59

British immigration law

Until 1971, British immigration legislation was piecemeal, various statutes having been introduced from as early as the 18th and 19th centuries to control the entry of foreigners. The 1962 Commonwealth Immigrants Act established immigration control on people from the British Commonwealth.[7] Commonwealth citizens had to obtain employment vouchers from the Ministry of Labour before being allowed to work, while aliens required work permits.

In 1968 the Labour government rushed through a second Commonwealth Immigrants Act, which cancelled commitments made by the previous Conservative Government, and withdrew the right to reside in Britain from many of those who were citizens of the United Kingdom and Colonies. In doing so, the Act changed the basis of immigration control. Whereas the crucial distinction had formerly been between 'aliens' and British subjects (including citizens of the Commonwealth countries), after 1968 only UK citizens with parents or grandparents born in Britain were not subject to British immigration control.

In 1971, a Conservative government incorporated and codified the main features of previous legislation, in the 1971 Immigration Act which introduced the notion of 'patriality'. 'Patrials', which included Commonwealth citizens with a parent born here, had the right of abode in the United Kingdom; but all aliens and non-patrial Commonwealth citizens could enter only with the permission of an immigration officer, who could refuse them entry and deport them or members of their family. In practice, this meant discriminating in favour of Canadians, New Zealanders, and Australians, against black British passport holders.

The bill also incorporated an administrative appeals system, first adopted in 1969. All appeals are heard in Britain, but people refused entry clearance abroad cannot come here, and those refused entry at the airport cannot stay here for the hearing unless they had obtained prior clearance from the British office responsible overseas.

A battery of criminal offences associated with illegal immigration was created. Illegal entry and overstaying became offences (Paragraph 24); so did assisting individuals to enter Britain illegally or harbouring them (Para. 25); or refusing to provide information and altering or making use of false documents (Para. 26). The immigration service was also given wider powers of control — to refuse entry, to impose conditions on entry, to remove illegal entrants and those refused entry by administrative order, and to arrest without a warrant anyone suspected of committing an offence under the Act.

These powers, which were formerly in the hands of the courts, were given under the Act to a far less accountable body — the immigration authorities.

The bill also established two separate but overlapping procedures for forcing people to leave the country:

Criminal proceedings. An individual arrested by the police and/or immigration service for committing an offence under the Act may be tried in a magistrates' court. If found guilty, magistrates may recommend deportation — a ruling which the Home Secretary may refuse to endorse. When criminal proceedings are involved, the accused can only appeal through normal court procedures. If the recommendation is carried out and a deportation order signed, it is not possible to challenge the deportation order itself on appeal, only to alter the destination to which the deportee will be sent.

Administrative order. The Home Office can also make an administrative decision to deport a person. It is possible to appeal against such decisions but the case does not go direct to court. An individual arrested by the police or immigration service as an illegal entrant may also be removed by administrative order. Under this procedure, the accused has no right of appeal at all in the United Kingdom, although appeals may be made from abroad. A case will be reviewed in British courts only if the alleged illegal entrant succeeds in applying for a judicial review. Alternatively, he or she may make direct representations to the Home Secretary through a member of the British Parliament.

The Immigration Act provides the legislative framework for the system of immigration control. The law is applied, however, through the 'Rules', which are as important as the Act because both have the force of law. Rules are laid before Parliament, and become law automatically unless a sufficient number of MPs 'pray' against them within 40 days (thereby forcing a debate). Unlike bills, Rules are not scrutinised in detail and can therefore be changed rather easily without fresh legislation. It is a facility which offers the Home Office many opportunities to define and extend its powers. The Rules on the entry of husbands and fiancés, for example, have been changed five times since 1972.

The Rules have been of crucial importance to Filipinos because courts decide, under the British system of law, how laws are to be interpreted. Although the courts are asked to define or restrict the powers of the Home Office and Immigration Service under the Act, in a number of crucial decisions on points of law, the courts accepted Home Office interpretations of the law and thereby increased the number of people against whom immigration officials can use their executive powers of removal.

The judgement of Azam (House of Lords, May 1973) established that the Immigration Act was applicable retrospectively. In the cases of Maqbool Hussain, Crown vs Bangoo and Safdar Hussain, it was accepted that entering by deception did constitute illegal entry. Choudhary (1978) and Morrow (1979) established that previous entry under false pretences invalidated the present stay, even if the circumstances were such that the person had become settled and had been in and out of the country during the same period. And following the decision on Claveria (1979), a work permit holder who obtained a permit on false pretences was defined as an illegal entrant, whether or not 'conditions' on their stay still applied.

Mrs Claveria is a Filipino who came to Britain in 1974 as a single person. In 1978, she became free to remain in Britain and applied for her husband to join her. Mr Claveria arrived at Heathrow in March 1978, but was refused permission to enter because the Home Office claimed his wife had entered by deception. The case went before the Divisional Court, which ruled in favour of the Home Office — so giving the Home Office the right to remove any person who had entered Britain in this way.

In the case of Zamir (House of Lords, 1980), Lord Justice Wilberforce ruled that an intending entrant owed 'a positive duty of candour to reveal all the relevant information', thereby making irrelevant the question of whether or not the entrant was conscious of a deception.

Since 1983, court rulings have slightly altered again. Following the cases of Khera and Khawaja (1983), it has been the responsibility of the Home Office to prove that deception was practised.

family of her unemployed brother. She has no prospect of saving enough to return home herself.

Another Filipino woman who came to Britain in 1974 sent every penny she earned as a resident domestic — then £18 per week — to pay her debt to the employment agency and help educate her younger brothers and sisters. She supported her own needs by working part-time in a hotel. Ten years later she had become a hospital auxiliary and was doing two additional part-time jobs to enable her to send £100 a month to her family.

Official and unofficial inquiries have clearly demonstrated that, in addition to exploiting the workers financially, many agencies failed to ensure that clients' papers were correctly drawn up. Although they appreciated how important it was to fulfil Department of Employment requirements, many did not fully inform their clients — and in some cases misinformed or positively misled them. As a result, some women applied for jobs in resident domestic work when they were married or separated and had families in the Philippines. In other cases, the references which applicants gave from their previous work experience were not related to the jobs in the catering and hotel trades for which they were applying. Agencies sometimes inserted references themselves, and some Filipinos found on their arrival in Britain that, although they had worked in hotels and restaurants in the Philippines and had given correct references, their agency had inserted references which were irrelevant or even false. As a result, the applications for work of a number of Filipinos were technically fraudulent.

Two standards

The British government was clearly aware of the extensive malpractices of recruitment agencies during the 1970s, when a large number of Filipinos came to Britain. The Minister of State at the Home Office made this clear. He wrote to *The Times* on 27 August 1980: 'The agencies played a large part in providing false information', and declared in Parliament on November 12 of the same year, 'Much has been said about the employment agencies. I do not seek to defend them generally. I do not argue that all of them behaved scrupulously — quite the opposite'.

However, it has suited the British authorities to relax or enforce the regulation of immigration in response to the demand for cheap labour. When demand was high during the 1970s the British Embassy in Manila and relevant ministries in London processed thousands of Philippine applications without excessive regard to the rules of entry.

Many Filipinos claim that the British Embassy in Manila never asked whether they were married or had children and at least one woman was granted a permit even though she stated quite clearly that she was married. During the early 1970s many Filipinos applied for, and received, tax allowances for their children living in the Philippines, and until 1979 the children of some domestic workers were allowed to join their parents in Britain.

Throughout the period, the British Embassy in Manila gave prospective workers no written information about work permit regulations or their

To keep the two full-time jobs she needs to make ends meet, this woman has to snatch what sleep she can during her night work

SORIN MASCA

importance under immigration law. In 1976 only 4.4% of the nearly eight thousand applications were refused — and all these cases were handled by just seven visa officers.[6]

With recession, however, this attitude changed. From 1979, visas were examined much more closely. It became difficult for Filipinos to secure jobs in Britain. The British government began a search for illegal entrants, and in 1981, after making inquiries in Britain and in the Philippines, the Home Office announced that it planned to remove 310 resident domestics who had allegedly concealed the existence of their children when applying for their work permits, and 90 hotel and catering staff whose work permits had allegedly been acquired on the basis of false references.

It is important to bear in mind that many of the British government's challenges were retrospective. In terms of justice, such a procedure is inherently unsatisfactory. It was all the more so in these cases, however, because the onus of proof lay with the migrants. It was sometimes impossible for restaurant workers, for example, to provide proof of their previous employment, because the Philippine restaurants which had employed them years before no longer existed.

Hospital workers

Practically all the Filipino migrants in the hospital service are women and work as resident domestics, auxiliary nurses or state enrolled nurses; some men are ward orderlies. Resident domestics clean the hospital wards, the kitchens, sitting rooms, and other patient areas. They also sweep, dust, and sterilise equipment, and wash up cutlery and dishes used by staff and patients. For a normal five-day week, working from 7.00 am to 3.30 pm, a resident domestic in 1985 earned about £45.00 (1985) after tax. Most take rooms in hostels provided by the hospital for £12 to £15 a week. The rent is automatically deducted from their wages. Hostels normally house 15-30 people. The bedrooms are usually very small with room for no more than a bed, a chair and a dressing table.

Rules are usually strict. Residents are not allowed to cook in their rooms, and since the kitchen and sitting room are often situated in the basement they have to walk down five or six flights of stairs to cook, then carry their food back to their rooms. Few kitchens are comfortable to eat in. Sitting rooms have a television and armchairs but they are also uninviting and rarely used except when the women have a party. All visitors are supposed to be out of the hostels by midnight.

Most resident domestics work many hours of overtime in the hospital, or take an additional part-time job. Although professionally trained and experienced, many Filipinos are treated with condescension by supervisors and do not feel appreciated. Practically all hospital resident domestics are members of a union.

In general, auxiliary nurses also live in nurses' homes or in hostels. Nurses' homes are generally better than hostels. The rooms are bigger and there is a kitchen and bathroom on each floor. Auxiliaries are more involved with the patients, since they wash and feed them and attend to their general

> 'I have always worked in a hotel since coming here in 1975, first as a chambermaid, then as a cashier. My weekly wage is £81.00 for a 40-hour week. I always split duty, 7.00am to 11 am and 12.30 to 4.30 pm, or 12 noon to 3.30 and 7.30 pm to midnight. It doesn't matter even if I work weekends or bank holidays, I never get any extra money, only time off when we're not too busy, and now that business is not so good I never get an opportunity to do overtime. I cannot get part-time work on a regular basis because of working split duties and irregular days off. We need to join a union, but in the hotel where I work we're not allowed to be in a union. Once when we were talking about joining a union we were all called together and told we're not allowed to join a union, that there is no need for unions in our hotel, and up until now nobody has joined.'

needs. Their work can be very demanding. Many Filipinos work with geriatrics in old people's homes and hospitals for the terminally ill. In the words of one nurse: 'After spending the day washing up after the patients, many of whom are incontinent,...my back aches, as I am always lifting them (...) but if I don't look after them what will they do?' In 1985 they earned £260 a month (£320 if they worked over week-ends). Many of the Filipino state-enrolled nurses also work with the very old.

Few Filipinos have achieved high positions within the British National Health Service, a very hierarchical institution in which rank is distinguished by style and colour of uniform as well as by privileges. A number of Filipinos originally came to Britain to train in the health service, for which they were required to have a university degree or teacher-training certificate. Very few have successfully moved on from being an auxiliary nurse or State Enrolled Nurse to become State Registered Nurses. Several factors may account for this.

The exam system has been criticised for failing a disproportionate number of English-speaking nurses from outside Britain because of the poor quality of their English. It is probable too that the levels of overtime put in by many Filipinos reduce their opportunities to study for higher qualifications.

Though many of the women feel a sense of belonging to their hospital or ward, they are also conscious that they are never likely to be promoted to ward sister — and that, if they return to the Philippines, their qualification as a state-enrolled nurse or auxiliary will not be recognised. They remain marginal to both the British health service and the nursing profession in their own country.

Hotel workers

'When I applied for this job,' said a Filipina waitress working in one hotel, 'they asked me if I was a member of a union. I said yes, and they said, 'Well, you don't need to apply here. We don't need the unions in this hotel; we treat our staff well.'

These women find it very difficult to make ends meet, but they are tied to

65

their jobs because of their living conditions. One is supporting six children in the Philippines. Another is a single parent, supporting her seven year old son and elderly parents. Living in hotel accommodation costs £20-25 a week for a very small room and conditions are generally bad. Working irregular hours in the job makes it difficult to get regular part-time work. Workers within the industry, including Filipinos, tend to move frequently.

The human cost of emigrating

The Filipinos who have come to work in Britain have made great sacrifices. To save money for their families, they work exceptionally long hours and do jobs which are badly paid, have little social prestige, and usually require skills far below those for which they are trained. More important than anything else, most of them are separated from their families, often for years at a time. The effects of this overwork and self-denial are felt both physically and socially.

As far as housing is concerned, many choose to save for their families rather than invest in housing for themselves. Because of their jobs, they can usually stay in hostels or in hotel accommodation provided by their employers. But the experience of living in such facilities for any length of time is both depressing and oppressive.

When they want me to do overtime, even on my day off — I might be asleep — they just phone through and ask me to work. Even if I am off sick, the supervisor comes to my room to check — she doesn't believe I am telling the truth. Women feel unable to invite friends, and feel perpetually under observation. Everybody knows everything about you... they know if we go out, or if we bring someone in, and I feel people are always gossiping about me. Sometimes I feel so lonely and isolated, even though there are plenty of people here. My room is so small and stuffy, but the bathroom is always so dirty, the toilet always out of order, but I cannot move out because I couldn't afford to pay travelling expenses if I move too far from my work.

The difficulties of finding alternative accommodation are compounded by low wages and by the fact that the local authority is not obliged to house single people and therefore provides little or no accommodation. London's Camden council has offered a flat-sharing arrangement.

It is difficult for most Filipinos to rent in the private sector — unless it is in the cheapest and therefore the worst kind of housing. One woman shared a small room with her two daughters on the sixth floor of an apartment block. On wet days the rain literally came through the roof and she collected it in a bucket. The only working toilet and bathroom were on the ground floor.

The physical health of many workers in the health service and hotel industry has also deteriorated, at least partly as a result of sustained overwork. Some Filipinos have now been in Britain for ten years or more, working up to 16 hours a day over long periods of time and doing jobs which require physical effort. Backache and pains in the legs, shoulders and arms are common complaints; many also suffer from heart problems and ulcers, and migraines. Some of these problems are clearly the result of environmental factors — long, unsocial hours, lack of proper food, and anxiety about their families at home and their insecure status in Britain. One woman with migraine was working for up to 100 hours a week doing three jobs, while another began work at 6.00am, had no breakfast, finished at 8.30pm — and by then was so tired that she rarely prepared a proper evening meal for herself. She suffered from dizzy spells, and, not surprisingly, declared, 'No matter how much rest or how many tonics I take, I still don't get my energy back.'

A high proportion of Filipinos in Britain suffer from depression. Between January 1979 and August 1982 the Filipino Chaplaincy in London helped 98 Filipino patients in psychiatric hospitals and another 649 outside hospital. One woman said:

I am pursued day and night thinking of my family at home. Even while I work my thoughts wander far and I spend my nights worrying or crying out of sheer helplessness (...) My husband seems to be cooling off, he seldom writes to me now (...) I sometimes get dizzy and often have stomach pains (...) My doctor says, 'Sorry but you must learn to live with it'. He gives me pills but they don't help.

Loneliness is also a considerable problem, particularly for women. Women who do not choose to marry in the Philippines have little prospect of finding a partner. Living in hostels with other women, working in the lowest paid sector of the economy, holding down a second or third job, they have few opportunities to meet eligible men.

Look at me now, I'm old already, and I still have to send £100 a month home to educate my nieces and nephews. How could I get married? (...) I got the opportunity to come to Britain and it is my duty to help my family.

Like Tess, some feel bitter that such a burden has been placed on them:

I get so tired all the time, it's only work, work, work, and now my family are asking for more money. I don't think I'll be able to keep going much longer... I'm not so young any more.

Even those women who are married to Filipino men, and who have qualified for residence, may experience difficulties. Immigration law discriminates against women. Until 1983 it permitted men to bring their wives to live with them in Britain but refused the same right to British women and women settled here. Many women therefore had to choose between their families and their jobs.[9]

This choice could be agonising. Rose decided after five years that she wished to return home to be with her children, who were entering their 'teens. But after nine months she was forced to come back to London: 'I couldn't find a job; the only thing to do was to come back here. I don't like it here, but at least I can ensure my children are fed and educated.'

Those who have successfully brought their children to live with them also discover problems. Having lived with grandparents or on their own, the children have grown apart and it is difficult for either parents or children to meet the expectations on both sides. The children also find that integration is difficult. They feel inferior at school, and parents find it hard to cope with looking after their children when they still need to work long or unsocial hours. They face the same problems in the Philippines, too. After five years in Britain, Tony and his wife returned to their two little girls, who had been aged two and three when they left. The girls ran away from him. 'You are not our papa,' they told him. 'He is in London.'

Culture

The great majority of Filipinos (more than 80%) are Catholics, and Filipinos in Britain celebrate the feasts of particular saints by making novenas. They hold bible studies and prayer meetings in thanksgiving for favours received, and also meet to commemorate the death or anniversary of parents or grandparents in the Philippines.

Many Filipinos also go on pilgrimages. About 400 travelled to Rome, Lourdes, Fatima and the Holy Land with the Filipino Chaplaincy in 1982, and most Filipinos will have been at least once to shrines in Britain like Walsingham.

These events are occasions for prayer, but also for celebration — to cook Filipino food, and to dance, sing and talk together with friends and family. Such meetings express a strong tradition of sharing between Filipinos. They are also essential for passing information about housing, jobs and travel, and for sending letters and gifts to the Philippines, the Middle East and other countries in Europe. When there is a bereavement, Filipinos donate generously to help send the body back to the Philippines to be buried in the family plot, or to help the family cope with expenses here.

Over the last few years, more formal cultural activities have greatly increased. There have always been beauty contests but several Filipino dance troupes have recently become popular attractions. The Kapiling Cultural Group performed in 1984 at the Labour Party Conference and several social events and meetings in London. A new cultural review *Tapayan Rebyu* also appeared in 1984, adding to several magazines which are regularly published by Philippine organisations or for migrants. The largest of these is *Pahayagan*, which is distributed throughout Europe and has an estimated readership of 20,000. *Kasama* is published by the Philippine Support Group in London.

The campaign against deportation

Given the decisions against Claveria and Zamir (see p.61), Filipinos under threat of removal had little chance of a successful appeal through judicial review. Nor could they appeal from within Britain. The only effective way of preventing immediate expulsion lay in direct appeals to the Home Secretary through members of parliament or trades union representatives. This

SORIN MASCA

procedure halted the process while the Home Secretary decided whether to exercise his discretion and permit the person concerned to remain. Coordinated by the Migrants Action Group, an energetic campaign was mounted on behalf of many individuals by Filipinos themselves, by MPs, trades unions, church officials and journalists.

Appeals to the Home Secretary do not challenge the legal basis of the decision, however, but are requests for leniency because of compassionate circumstances or other mitigating factors. The situation was such that injustices and inconsistencies were certain to occur. Ministers claimed to look at each case on its merits with 'full regard to compassionate circumstances within the context of our overall responsibility to maintain a firm and effective control over immigration'. Nevertheless a number of Filipinos and their families were forcibly removed for technical or unwitting infringement of the law, often after they had worked and paid taxes in Britain for a period of several years, while others were permitted to remain even though their circumstances were apparently very similar.

Length of stay. In allowing one Filipina to remain, the Home Office referred to the length of time (ten years) she had been in the United Kingdom. However, among those refused were one man who had lived nine and a half years in Britain, and three who had worked in Britain for eight years. All of them had spent long periods in full employment on low wages.[8]

Dependants in the Philippines. One person who was allowed to stay had

69

eleven dependants; another had two sisters with eight dependants. Some of those who were removed however, also supported many relatives. One supported ten, including two aged parents; another had a dependent son and partially dependent parents plus a sister and three children. Nor does it appear that the decision was based on a combination of length of stay and the presence of dependants in the Philippines, since the first of those removed had lived in Britain for five years and the second seven, whereas those who were allowed to stay had lived in the country for six and five years respectively.

Links with the United Kingdom. This relates mainly to those whose children were born in Britain and of 12 such cases seven were allowed to remain. These included three married couples, five of whom had no dependants in the Philippines. Two successful applicants had been in the United Kingdom for eight years, one for five years and the others for between two to four years. Of those refused permission to stay, one had lived for nine and a half years in Britain and had a child born there, while another couple, whose child had also been born in Britain, had spent four and six years respectively in the United Kingdom and had four dependants in the Philippines.

Work experience. Of those allowed to remain, ten had no work experience and three had received training from the agencies which recruited them. Of those refused, nine continued to deny there had been deception and at least two had received several months training. A Miss P. had experience as a part-time worker in the Philippine restaurant of a relative and, after being refused several times, she was finally allowed to stay; but although Mrs. C. had worked for many years in her family's restaurant, she was removed. All of these people were highly recommended by their employers, who wrote to the Home Office in their support.

The criteria on which ministers based their judgement thus appeared to be arbitrary, reinforcing the view that persistent lobbying rather than the quality of evidence was the decisive factor. Of the 400 people threatened with removal, the majority were permitted to remain after representations, but more than 100 were removed, or gave up and returned to the Philippines or found jobs in other countries.

Perhaps the most disturbing feature of the removals is that many Filipinos were forcibly repatriated without regard or concern for the fact that they had worked in Britain for up to ten years. Although they had paid taxes and fulfilled all their legal obligations while working, they were not considered to have acquired any rights in consequence.

One Filipino came to Britain in 1974 to work as a resident domestic for the owner of a small hotel. His reliability and capacity were such that a few years later his employer appointed him manager. The man supported his wife and six children in the Philippines. Every month he sent his salary to his family, retaining pocket money for himself. In 1979 three of his children were in college, two were in high school, and the youngest was in junior school.

In that year, he received a letter from the Home Office telling him that he was here illegally and that he would have to return to the Philippines. The man claimed consistently that when he applied to work in Britain as a resident domestic he did not know he was ineligible. He was among those who applied for, and received tax allowance for his children in the early seventies.

Though his employer wrote on his behalf and many representations were made, he was removed to the Philippines in March 1981. During the seven years he lived in Britain he had paid at least £14,000 in tax and insurance, without receiving any benefits either for himself or his family. Since his return, his children have had to give up their education, he himself has been ill and the cost of his hospital treatment has exhausted the family's savings. In a letter, he wrote: 'I am now a broken man.'

SORIN MASCA

71

FEDERAL REPUBLIC OF GERMANY

The first Filipinos recruited to work in Germany arrived in the early 1960s. Most were employed in hospitals, on contracts arranged by town and city administrations. Like employees from other Asian countries, Filipino professionals normally have a three-year contract and are granted residence permits to cover their period of employment. Nursing staff, who are badly needed in hospitals, may renew their contract for a further one or two years, but there is no guarantee that applications will be accepted.

On average Filipinos remain in Germany for five years. Through their employer, some have been able to secure an official contract of employment. This is difficult, however, because a residence permit is required before a contract will be issued, and these are only provided by the agency for alien registration if 'the interests of the Federal Republic of Germany are not impaired'. Filipinos who have worked for five years in Germany have a legal right to extend their contract, regardless of the situation in the labour market. To do so, however, they again need a residence permit. Since 1976 it has become very difficult for foreigners to enter Germany, though policies do vary from one federal state to another. Since the Ministry of the Interior has not issued specific guidelines regarding the status of aliens, much depends upon the discretionary decisions of individual immigration officers, as in the United Kingdom.

A Filipino who marries another Philippine citizen is not entitled to bring his or her partner back to Germany. Parents are not entitled to bring their children or other family members.

Isolation and stress are problems as they are in other European countries. Integration is difficult and there is a relatively high incidence of depression and psychological breakdown, including suicide. Unable to speak the language and quite unprepared for European society, many Filipinos in Germany hardly come into contact with Germans and, insecure and isolated, form 'Filipino ghettos'. In addition to being paid lower wages, Filipinos are often treated with condescension by their German colleagues and asked to do more unpleasant work or longer hours.

Nurses began to arrive in large numbers after 1968, and initially there were problems with the recruitment practices of private agencies, which charged inflated fees. In order to stop abuses, the Association of German Hospitals and the Philippine Government therefore agreed in 1974 that the Overseas Employment Development Board (OEDB) would take responsibility for all recruitment, and would additionally provide a two-month induction course in German and German life. These courses never took place because German hospitals ceased to recruit Filipinos in 1976.

In 1974 the German branch of Caritas funded two social workers to advise Filipinos in Cologne and Stuttgart. The office in Cologne remains open.

Although most Filipina nurses and midwives who wished to do so have been able to renew their contracts, many nurses have returned to the Philippines or moved to jobs in other countries — some as the wives of American soldiers. The number of nurses has declined from 3,500 in 1976 to about 1,500 in 1982. Many Filipinas are now working in psychiatric hospitals and homes for the very old, which find it difficult to recruit German staff. About 700 Filipinos are also employed in Bonn as servants, drivers or typists working for embassy staff. A number are also employed at the American embassy. It is not possible to assess how many Filipinos are living illegally in Germany.

Like Holland and Britain, Germany has a Philippine 'brides' market. Since 1976 many Filipinas have accepted written or oral promises of marriage from German men, often passed on by German intermediaries or agencies which offer the 'brides' virtually no protection from abuse. Many German newspapers and magazines carry advertisements promoting Philippine women — usually described as sweet, submissive, exotic beauties, or alternatively as willing and efficient domestic workers.

In many cases, the man concerned does not even expect to marry the woman immediately, but lives with her on the assumption that if she is found not to be acceptable to him, he may send her back. Predictably, there are frequent problems of communication and differing expectations on both sides.

In 1982 there were some 9,500 Filipinos living in Germany, over 70% of whom were women. Approximately 40% of the total community were married.

FRANCE

There is a relatively small Filipino community in France, about half of whom came into the country following the Iranian revolution in 1979. The majority are women, working as domestic servants for French and expatriate employers. Until 1982, when the Socialist government declared an amnesty, all were illegal residents. Since then, more have continued to filter into the country, and these are liable to be deported.

ITALY

Filipinos began migrating to Italy in the early 1970s. At that time, immigration controls were lax, and most registered as tourists and sought work afterwards. Only a few arrived with contracts. After 1978 this movement became more organised, and agencies in the Philippines began to arrange tourist papers for migrant workers. In an attempt to regulate the number of illegal entries and control abuses, the Italian government in 1982 imposed stricter penalties on employers and declared an amnesty to all foreign workers who had entered Italy before December 31, 1981. Large numbers of Filipinos still enter Italy illegally, however, and many continue to pay agency fees of up to 40,000 lira (US$29 in 1986) in order to do so. It is estimated that about three quarters of the Filipinos living in Italy are there illegally.

It is, therefore, very difficult to ascertain how many Filipinos there are in the country, but there are believed to be at least 30,000 and possibly up to 50,000. Many have moved on from Italy to other countries — particularly Canada, the United States and Spain, and also Libya and Nigeria.

Up to 90% of Filipinos in Italy are women. Most have college or

73

secondary education. In the early years the majority of migrants were professionally skilled, although towards the end of the 1970s greater numbers of factory workers began to enter the country.

Filipinos do a range of jobs in Italy — as hospital aides and nurses, chauffeurs and hotel workers. Some work in the entertainment business, particularly in Naples. By far the largest number, however, are employed in domestic service. Domestic workers under contract earn a minimum wage of US$200 per month. Those working illegally, who usually work part-time for several employers, earn more (Lira 4,500-6,000 per hour in 1985, US$2.40-3.20) but are usually uninsured. Contracts negotiated in Italy usually stipulate a minimum wage, last for one year and are renewable. Conditions vary, but under Italian law Filipino workers have the right to join unions and to receive equal treatment with Italians. Those with regular contracts are entitled to health insurance, while those who work illegally are generally treated by the employer's doctor. Employees have statutory rights to holidays.

As in other countries, Filipinos are nevertheless vulnerable to exploitation, and may have great difficulties in transferring to a new job if their employer is reluctant to let them go. Without their passport and other papers, and a letter from their previous employer, a domestic worker cannot legally be taken on by a new employer. As a result, domestics may be stranded between jobs for periods of several months. Some have been arrested for drug trafficking, and Italian newspapers regularly report cases of personal tragedy — suicide, the murder of one Filipino by another, the case of a mother who killed her own child to avoid disgrace. Others have drifted into crime and prostitution, in many cases because they have been unable to find regular work or sort out their legal status.

Workers who have taken regular contracts in the Philippines through government agencies such as the OEDB are often financially in a worse position than workers who have found jobs through the black market. Their contract does not allow them to change their employer, and they are paid as little as a third of those working illegally.

The Philippine Embassy in Italy has also tried to apply Executive Order 857 to Filipinos in Italy and, as in other countries, has refused to process papers or renew the passports of those who have not remitted 50% or more of their income through the Philippine banking system. In cases of distress — when Filipinos have been stranded, have had to be repatriated for medical reasons or have died — the Embassy has generally been unable to provide real assistance.

THE NETHERLANDS

Beginning in 1964, several groups of Filipina nurses worked in Rotterdam and Leiden, then from 1967 in Amsterdam, Eindhoven, Bussum and Heerenveen. The contracts were arranged through Dutch missionaries in the Philippines. On the whole they enjoyed reasonable salaries and living conditions. Since 1976 groups of Filipinas have worked in Appeldoorn, Utrecht and other Dutch cities.

In 1964 and again in 1975 two batches of 100-150 factory workers came to Holland on contracts which were also arranged through Dutch missionaries. They worked at the Berghaus textiles company until this closed down, after which most of the workers migrated to Canada.

Most of the first factory workers came from rural areas. A major problem was loneliness and a decision to house them together in apartments compounded their troubles. This 'community' system created sexual problems and a social worker was hired, unsuccessfully, to help sort out their difficulties. Economically, on the other hand, although they received lower wages than their Dutch colleagues, they generally accepted the terms offered because they were so much better than they would have received at home.

Nurses also found adaptation difficult. This was partly because they did not speak Dutch and because loneliness and homesickness were common. The Filipina nurses also resented doing dirty jobs which they were not expected to perform in the Philippines and this aroused the resentment of Dutch staff. In general, however, the Filipina nurses provided a valuable service without complaint and, as in other countries, accepted overtime as well as evening and weekend duties.

Most of the nurses who arrived before 1972 eventually returned home, though some of the workers and nurses married men they met in Holland. After martial law was introduced in the Philippines, more professional and skilled workers arrived, escaping from political repression and the lack of economic opportunities at home. In addition to nurses and factory workers, entertainers, dancers and singers now tour regularly and some Filipinas work as domestic helpers. Of the 700 Filipinos now officially resident in Holland, about 100 are students, most of whom are government employees sponsored by the Dutch government. No new contracts for nurses have been signed in recent years.

SPAIN

There are more than 50,000 Filipinos in Spain, of whom 30,000 live in Madrid. There are large groups in Barcelona, Valencia and Bilbao. About 90% of the migrant workers are women, and roughly 80% have degrees or have studied in college. Almost all work either as domestic helpers or in the restaurant trade.

Live-in domestic helpers (*internas*) work very long hours — at least 16 hours a day — and earn on average 30,000 pesetas a month (about $180). There are no laws in Spain governing the employment of domestic workers, and their conditions therefore depend upon the arrangements they are able to make with their employers. Most domestic helpers in 1985 would consider their employer had made a good offer if pay amounted to at least 30,000 pesetas, and included double pay for two months, one month's paid vacation, and social security cover. Very few enjoy all these benefits, however. Those who 'live out' (*externas*) earn more or less the same salary as *internas* but work fewer hours — about eight per day. They have the advantage of being able to take a second or third job and can feel they are

75

employees rather than servants. On the other hand, they have to pay for their board and lodging, clothes and transportation.

Restaurant workers — of whom the majority are waiters and cooks — earn between 40,000 and 50,000 pesetas monthly. Many work in Chinese restaurants whose owners rarely take the trouble to process employees' papers. As a result most Filipino restaurant workers make arrangements with Spanish friends, who give them contracts as 'domestic workers' in order to get them residence certificates. A number of Filipinos work in private service as *matrimonio* (a couple) with their wives or girlfriends.

A large number of Filipinos have recently been deported because their papers were not in order. They are also victims of unscrupulous recruitment agencies, which issue false Spanish visas in Manila, and advertise jobs under false premises. Some Filipinos have had to pay the cost of their airfare to Spain twice over, first to the reception agent in Spain, and then to the employer who had really advanced the money.

SWEDEN

The first Filipinos in Sweden replaced local people as domestic workers in the 1960s. In the early 1970s a number of seamen also settled with their families in the area of Göteborg. Some of the wives of Swedish men have trained and now work as orderlies or nurses' aides in hospitals and nursing homes.

There has also been a steady trickle of Filipinos to embassies in Stockholm. The overwhelming majority work as domestics in the families of embassy personnel. They are generally the most exploited group, because they can remain in Sweden only on the basis of certificates issued by their employers. They tend to receive the lowest wages and work the longest hours, and are not covered by Swedish social security benefits or sickness insurance.

Following the worldwide economic recession in the early 1970s Swedish immigration rules became stricter. Since 1981 all applications must be made in the Philippines and applicants are accepted only if they can prove they have a job in Sweden. These regulations have been by-passed in some cases. A number of Filipinos have been able to bring over their relatives on three-month tourist visas and then found jobs for them with embassies in Stockholm. The most recent entrants included wives of Iranian refugees.

Legal immigrants are entitled on their arrival to at least 250 hours of Swedish language training and job training for up to a year.

At the end of 1984 there were 700 Filipinos in the country (excluding naturalised Swedes).

7. THE MIDDLE EAST

'Here in Riyadh, almost half the foreigners are Filipino. Everywhere you look there are Filipinos, from the smallest company and maybe up to the government offices there are Filipinos.'

A worker in Riyadh.

As a direct result of the oil construction boom which followed the sudden increase in the price of Arab oil, during the mid-1970s the Middle East became the main source of employment for migrant workers from Asia. In 1983 alone, approximately 300,000 Filipinos, earning about US$1 billion in foreign currency for the national economy, were employed in the Middle East. For several years, the area has also been the largest market for Filipino contractors.

For all its importance, nevertheless, little has been written about the living and working conditions which Filipinos experience. This chapter focuses particularly on Saudi Arabia, where by far the largest number of Filipinos are employed, followed by Kuwait, the United Arab Emirates, Libya, and Iraq.

The Arab connection: paving the way to modernisation and exploitation

The Middle East has a total land area of about 4,500,000 square kilometres and is roughly sixty times the area of the Philippines. It is the centre of Islam. As a result, the lives of Filipino contract workers in most of the Arab states are subject to Islamic law and Arab culture. No one is exempted, including aliens from distinctly different cultures and societies. Even in Kuwait, for example, where almost 70% of the population are non-Kuwaitis, foreigners are approached with suspicion and disdain. The employment of expatriates is limited to service and non-essential sectors. Moreover, migrant workers do not have any political rights and are particularly vulnerable to exploitation by the foreign contractors and companies which hire them.[1]

Arab oil revenues rose from US$80 bn in the decade preceding 1973 to US$700 bn between 1973 and 1978. In some countries — such as Iran — oil revenues after 1973 doubled the gross national product.

The increase in income stimulated a large boom in development projects which helped cause imports to OPEC countries to increase sharply, by an average of 60% in the first five years after 1973. Over the same period, these imports represented about 75% of OPEC oil revenues.

Labour migration in the Middle East

Charles Keely argued that Arab countries employed Asian workers for four main reasons.[2] They wanted, first of all, to reduce the risks of depending on a single source or cartel. Secondly, most of the Middle Eastern countries which import labour are conservative monarchies, preoccupied by questions of security. Since the Arab countries with a labour surplus often have, like Egypt, a more socialist or radical tradition, they preferred not to rely on these sources alone. Thirdly, it is rather easier to make sure that Asians remain 'temporary' workers, because they are unable to integrate into Middle Eastern societies like Arab migrant workers. Finally, Asian labour is simply much cheaper. They not only work for lower wages than other expatriates, but are relatively productive, and, being migrants, leave their families behind and do not require the support of costly health and education services.

For Filipinos, Saudi Arabia has come to symbolise labour migration in all forms. *Katas ng Saudi* ('Saudi Juice') is a new path to prosperity. 'This "Saudi Juice" has really helped our country a lot…Many things have changed in our lives. Before, only the rich can afford to eat good food. Now, the rich can be equalled by someone who has gone to Saudi Arabia.'[3]

In 1976 the Philippine Bureau of Employment Services (BES) and the Overseas Employment Development Board (OEDB) altogether recruited some 4,970 Filipino workers for the Middle East. This represented 26% of all workers processed by these government agencies. By 1979 the proportion had increased to 63% and by 1983 more than 83% of all Filipino migrant workers were going to the Middle East. Unofficial figures collected by the Saudi authorities suggested that, in 1982, 180,000 Filipinos were working in Saudi Arabia alone.[4]

Saudi Arabia is by far the largest employer. Iraq, Kuwait, the United Arab Emirates and Libya each employed over 10,000 workers in 1983.

Table 2: Distribution of Filipino Migrant Workers in the Middle East by Country of Destination (as processed by BES, OEDB and POEA)

Country	1976	1979	1982	1983	% in Region 1983
UAE	5	2,269	7,762	12,831	4.0
Bahrain	302	1,069	3,910	6,617	2.1
Iran	6	—	10	193	0.06
Iraq	—	1,093	20,219	14,349	4.5
Israel	2	44	—	8	—
Jordan	2	50	2,803	1,875	0.6
Kuwait	20	2,583	8,604	14,781	4.6
Libya	—	111	6,991	11,042	3.44
Oman	—	57	1,648	2,773	0.8
Qatar	—	979	1,357	2,863	0.9
Saudi Arabia	4,633	49,854	156,496	253,080	79.0
Total	4,970	58,109	209,800	320,412	100.00

Sources:
1976-79: *Bureau of Employment Services Annual Report 1979*, BES, MOLE, Philippines, 1979, p.7.
1982: *Philippine Overseas Employment Administration Annual Report 1983*, POEA, MOLE, Philippines, 1982, p.23.
1983: *POEA Annual Report 1983*, POEA, MOLE, Philippines, 1983, p.28.

The great majority (71%) were employed in construction or construction-related industries as labourers, plumbers, welders, transport equipment operators, bricklayers and carpenters. Cooks, housekeepers and managers in the catering and lodging industries made up the second largest category (12%), followed by clerical staff (4.2%), who were mainly secretaries and bookkeepers.

Table 3 demonstrates that the great majority of Filipinos going to the Gulf region were semi-skilled and skilled workers. The vast majority — about 80% — were male.

Table 3: Occupational Distribution of Filipino Workers in the Middle East (as a proportion of registered overseas employment 1983)

Occupational Grouping	Number in each category	as% of ME total	as % of each category Worldwide
Professions, Technical and Related Workers	34,165	10.6	65
Administrative, Executive, Managerial & Related Workers	1,586	0.5	85
Clerical	13,587	4.2	96
Sales	1,987	0.6	88
Service	39,429	12.3	68
Construction	231,152	72.0	93
Agriculture	1,508	0.4	92
Total	320,412		

Source: *POEA Annual Report 1983*, MOLE, Philippines, 1983, p. 27.

Working conditions and wages

Both skilled and unskilled workers in the Middle East generally earn between four and five times more than they would in the Philippines. Foremen and supervisors earn from two to three times more and executives about twice the Philippines rate.[5]

In 1982, the Philippine Overseas Employment Administration (POEA) found that a non-skilled worker received on average a basic wage of US$208 to US$300 a month, when the Philippine minimum wage stood at US$87 per month.[6] Some companies pay more. In 1985 the French construction and public works multinational, Dumez, which employs some 12,000 Filipinos in various projects in the Middle East, was paying on average a basic salary of $384 a month.[7]

Overseas workers nevertheless face extensive discrimination. Wage levels are set according to nationality and religion rather than skill, and at least three general payrolls are maintained. Americans and Europeans are paid the most, followed by the local nationals. Nationals from the Philippines and other countries in Asia are paid the lowest rate.[8]

For Filipinos the differential has recently grown larger, as wages have been driven down by the combined effects of the world recession, which has reduced the demand for workers, and the Philippines domestic crisis, which increased the supply of Filipinos seeking work overseas. Faced with intense competition, recruiting agencies have secured contracts by offering cheaper workers. 'The latest here (in Saudi) is that new recruits get lower wages. Its all the agency's fault, they bid against one another and whoever bids the lowest is the one chosen by the Arab.'

In most cases, however, living and working conditions, though hard, are tolerable. In most private enterprises, work begins at 9 am and continues until 2 pm, and then from 4 pm until 8 pm after a two-hour break for lunch. Overtime is paid at time-and-a-half and rest days and holidays at double pay. A normal weekend begins on Thursday at noon and ends on Friday evening, work resuming on Saturday morning. The normal schedule changes during Ramadan and Haj when Muslim workers have daily prayer intervals or breaks during the period.[9]

Contract violations and other abuses

There have been many cases of abuses. Employers have changed the terms of contracts, have failed to provide promised living and working conditions and have recruited or fired employees illegally. In one far from unusual case, nine nurses were recruited by Filipinas-Arabian Resources Incorporated (FARI) to work at the Dr. M. Erfan Hospital in Jeddah, Saudi Arabia, in December 1983. In the following March, they surrendered their *iquamas* or residence certificates on being told it was 'normal procedure' to do so, and were then made redundant because, according to their employers, they were not qualified for their positions. The letters they received were undated and issued four months after they had begun working at the hospital and one month after their three-month probationary period had ended.

In 1982, Mr. Diosdado Claceto, a 42-year-old steel fixer from Pampanga,

Construction sites often lack safety provision

was injured together with eleven co-workers when the company truck in which they were riding overturned while taking him to his jobsite. Mr Claceto sustained a fracture and could not work. He was refused the medical benefits due to him, including sick leave and vacation or repatriation and his employer, Al-Mobty Establishment for Trading and Construction, ordered him to stay on for another month after his contract expired in October 1982. During this period he was not given food allowances, and had to depend on the assistance of other Filipinos. He returned to the Philippines and, through Kaibigan, filed a case in the POEA against the employer and recruitment agency.

Others have been summarily reprimanded or illegally deported. Fernando de Guzman was made to sign a blank contract when he reached his jobsite in Saudi Arabia. He complained about this anomaly and, when the employer persisted, boycotted his job. He was then deported by his employer, Cannonball Engineering and Construction Inc., for 'insubordination', and filed a case against both the employer and the agency that recruited him.

In another case, 208 workers in Iraq abandoned their jobs after salaries had not been paid and grave threats by the company's security personnel. The workers sought refuge at the Philippine Embassy where they filed their request for repatriation to Manila.[10]

Failure to pay salaries and benefits is not confined to foreign construction companies. The Philippine National Construction Corporation (formerly

Living quarters for migrants in the Middle East

the Construction and Development Corporation of the Philippines) — described by a highranking Iraqi official as 'inefficient and unproductive in its operations'[11] — failed for six months to transfer the remittances of its employees in projects in Saudi Arabia and Iraq and in some countries in South-East Asia.

Even major contracting companies have failed to honour contracts, particularly after 1982 when recession struck the construction industry. Carlson Al Saudia, a Saudi-American contractor, abandoned its projects in Saudi Arabia in 1984, leaving 3,000 Filipino, Pakistani, British and American workers stranded without pay.[12] Some of these workers were reported to have had to sell their blood to raise money to buy food.[13]

Claiming late payment by its Saudi clients, the Construction and Development Corporation of the Philippines (CDCP) also failed to pay wages to hundreds of its Filipino workers in Saudi Arabia in 1984.

Living conditions

Medical and dental facilities are provided by large companies such as ARAMCO and Dumez. Employees have access to free medicine, hospitalisation and other social benefits. They are usually entitled to an insurance policy (with a value of 5,000-10,000 pesos) which includes life cover and cover against sickness and war risk.[14]

In general the larger companies also provide comfortable living quarters, with air-conditioning, washing facilities, and access to sports facilities

83

(swimming pools, basketball, squash).[15] The OEDB reported in 1982 that workers 'enjoy adequately comfortable housing facilities where field workers assigned in the desert live in camps or trailers housing six to eight men (...) food is good and mess halls are generally clean and well equipped.'[16]

Nevertheless conditions are not always so good. Big companies employ only a small fraction of the total Filipino workforce and, according to one study, many of the smaller companies 'provide workers with the most basic facilities and amenities such as bunk beds and electric fans (...) more people share each room and bath (...) and seldom are workers provided with sports and recreation facilities'.[17]

Campsites in the desert are often isolated and workers more frequently encounter delays in payment, remittance problems, and contract violations. In many cases, they have little or no hope of legal redress when abuses do take place.

The environment itself causes great stress. In some desert areas temperatures rise to 135° Fahrenheit during the summer. Water may be scarce. Food, when it is provided, is often very dull, and based entirely on poultry for months at a time: eggs for breakfast, chicken for lunch and chicken for dinner.

Social barriers in the Arab states

The problems of being away from home are exacerbated by the differences in cultural attitudes in the Middle East which give rise to bias and discrimination. As one man working in Saudi Arabia described it:

Some Arabs can be good friends to Filipinos, especially those who have studied and visited our country. But there are some who look at Filipinos differently. Here in our company, though, Saudi Telephone, they treat us okay. What can't be taken away is the bias because in our department there are many foreigners, Egyptians and Pakistanis. I'm not being boastful but we receive less compared to them even though we know more about the job. It's because their religion is the same with the Arabs — they are Muslims, and another advantage that they have is that they know and speak Arabic, the national language here in Saudi Arabia.

Discrimination — which is a marked feature of Western expatriate attitudes as well as of attitudes among the local communities — is strongly resented: 'Here you'll really eat your pride. You can't say a thing. When they speak, you can't do anything about it, you're in their country. If it were not for the dollar, I don't know if anyone would want to work here anymore.'

It is not surprising that fights break out between workers or that there is often tension between workers of different nationalities.

Workers find different ways of dealing with the serious problems of homesickness and boredom. The very restrictive moral values of Saudi Arabia and some of the other Middle Eastern societies mean that workers have to forego, at least in public, many of their pleasures, including drinking

The slogan reads: 'Prison without bars'

and gambling, which are prohibited by Arab law.

Sexual attitudes are very different and can lead to serious misunderstanding or problems. As one worker commented:

> The Arabs are very strict, especially on women. Brother, it's true here · that the women have veils. Even Filipinas are required to wear their black clothes like toga whenever they go out. And you can't really stare at the girls here, it's forbidden. They really follow God's Commandment that if you look at a girl with lust or desire you have already sinned, a sin of adultery.

Nonetheless, some migrants run prostitution rackets. Illicit alcohol is produced, and gambling is all-pervasive in the privacy of the workers' barracks, where cards are smuggled in and every conceivable form of betting scheme can be found. Gambling has frequently caused tragedy for workers who have lost all their earnings and have been unable to send anything home to their families.

One common way of passing the time is window shopping at the supermarkets, which abound in major cities. Another is watching videos, which are cheap and make up for the absence of cinemas. Masses are offered on Fridays in some embassies (among them the US, British and Venezuelan) and there is a Catholic church in Manama, the capital city of Bahrain.

'Islamic justice'

The price of being caught infringing Saudi laws is high. Filipinos as well as other nationals have been fired, deported and even jailed for minor misdemeanours, including car accidents. That 'Islamic justice' can also be brutal was shown by the well-publicised case of Conrado Acosta and Mano Mixtang, who were beheaded in 1982. Accused of rape and robbery, the two were immediately sentenced and executed, though a Filipino who was in Saudi Arabia at the time reported that they had robbed the Arab couple who employed them in order to get even with the husband, who, it was alleged, had raped the wife of one Filipino in front of him.[18] Other crimes like shoplifting can be punished by severing a finger. Prisoners found guilty of crimes such as physical assault are sentenced to be lashed.

Labour relations

In spite of the strict ban against such actions Filipinos have been involved in numerous strikes, boycotts, work stoppages and other forms of mass action in protest against contract violations, exploitation and other abuses.

In 1985 only three embassy attachés and two POEA representatives were serving the needs of the 300,000 Filipinos employed throughout the region. Every day they received between 50 and 200 calls for help in solving labour problems ranging from non-payment of wages and benefits to mistreatment and illegal sacking.[19] In addition, they were expected by the government 'to coordinate all labor training, employment and workers' welfare functions and operations from offices in Jeddah, Saudi Arabia (...) promote Filipino manpower and expertise (...) and maximise foreign exchange generation.'[20] This small office is clearly unable to provide assistance where it was needed and the staff usually offered only to arbitrate.

In spite of the scale of organised labour movement into the Middle East and the foreign exchange income it generates, the Philippine government had not, during the Marcos period, negotiated one bilateral agreement with any Middle Eastern government to protect and formalise the rights of its citizens while they were in the region. The government concentrated instead on improving the deployment of workers in the Middle East — in other words maintaining the flow 'of skills and expertise to the Kingdom', as Mr Blas Ople described it when he visited Saudi Arabia as Philippine Minister of Labor in 1983.

Since 1985 the language of expansion has no longer been appropriate. The demand for labour in the Middle East has recently shifted away from construction workers to managerial and maintenance staff — and since more than 90% of Filipinos in the Middle East are construction workers, this means drastic change for the government's labour export programme as well as for the workers themselves. There are clear signs that the great investment boom in the Arab economies is coming to an end and that Filipinos must expect a relative decline in the overall demand for their labour. It may well be that the long-term result of the government's drive to export workers to the Middle East will be to create a large pool of skilled workers, used to earning good wages, who will have no hope of finding work when they flow back into a domestic economy that is unable to receive them.

8. ASIA-PACIFIC REGION

'Loneliness is there. When you think of home you have to think of the situation... So I guess it is worth staying: the pay is much better... The happiness there is very different from the happiness here. It seems here it is just a quarter of the happiness I enjoyed in the Philippines. There is no place like home.'
A domestic worker in Hong Kong, 1984

In Japanese night clubs, in the oil-fields of Brunei, in households all over Hong Kong, there are Filipinos working hard to earn precious dollars for their families.

Filipinos have emigrated for many years to other Asian countries. In the 1960's they toiled in the construction sites of Vietnam, Thailand and Guam, and a number worked as loggers in the forests of Indonesia. In Japan, Hong Kong and other southeast Asian countries, even before the second world war, Filipino entertainers were seen to be the 'entertainers of Asia'.

Asian development and labour migration

A glance at the economies of SE Asia reveals great disparities in their growth. Japan and Australia are industrial powers. Hong Kong and Singapore have become rich trading and financial centres for Asia and the West. Taiwan, Korea, and New Zealand are in various stages of intermediary development. And Brunei, though it has only recently gained its independence, is a large oil and gas exporter and one of the richest countries in the region.

The others, including the Philippines, are less developed and offer their peoples a poorer standard of living. They share high unemployment, a balance of payments deficit, and huge foreign debts. Their peoples are poor and many suffer from extreme poverty.

The new international division of labour which is emerging, and which is sharply influencing the outlook for less developed countries, results from the uneven economic development which has been an increasingly evident feature of the world economy. The export-oriented, import-dependent economies of less-developed countries have created massive labour displacements, causing not only rural to urban migration but also migration from one country to another. Filipinos migrate to Malaysia, Malaysians to Indonesia, Indonesians to Malaysia, and so on. For the most part, this movement is essentially a question of getting a little more to eat.

AUSTRALIA

Until recently it was extremely difficult for non-Caucasians to settle in Australia, and Filipinos began going there only in the 1970s. Initially most were businessmen and professionals. About 5,000 of the 7,000 registered immigrants entering Australia annually from Asia are Filipinos.

By far the largest number, however, have been women who have entered

the country to become brides of Australian men. Australia is one of the centres of a growing trade in Filipino (and Thai) women. It is disturbing not only because of the numbers of women involved — at least 8,000 a year in Australia during the early 1980s — but also because it has become an increasingly organised business. As in West Germany, Holland, Britain, the United States and other western countries, private companies have been formed to advertise 'bride lists' and arrange marriages with Filipinas for their male clients.

There is virtually no effective regulation of this business, which is open to the worst kinds of abuses. Philippine newspapers like *Bulletin Today* regularly carry advertisements on behalf of agencies or individuals, and the women themselves have very little protection. 'In Germany, many of the Filipinas who hoped to settle down ended up as prostitutes with their husbands as pimps.' 'I expect my wife to earn for me for the next ten years at least $4,000 a month,' said a German who paid $5,000 for his Filipina wife. In another case, the German husband of a Filipina mail-order bride reportedly 'shared' her with some of his friends to compensate for her travel expenses which the men had pooled together (...) One hopeful Filipino woman was murdered by her Australian husband who had her cremated after collecting insurance money on her life.'

These are the horror stories. Even when the brides are not criminally abused or exploited, however, the record suggests that a high proportion of the relationships fail. Many of the men involved are on average ten or twenty years older than their wives and others expect their partners to act in a

In London a middle-aged man approaches a marriage bureau to help him find a wife. Upon payment of an agency fee of £95, he is given a sheaf of hundreds of photographs of beautiful Filipino women from which to take his pick.

Halfway across the globe, in Sydney, a lonely elderly Australian in search of a lifetime partner goes to a matchmaking agency. For an A$85-a-year membership fee, he can get himself introduced by mail to as many Filipino women as possible. And for an additional $145, he even gets to see these women on video.

In California, an American can avail himself of the services of an 'introduction agency'. For only US$90 a year, he is entitled to a catalogue of beautiful Asian women, most of them Filipinas, complete with names, addresses and other details.

From. Luz V del Hosario, *Problem or Solution? Mail Order Brides*, in Pinoy Overseas Chronicle, Nov 1985.

stereotypically submissive way. A large number of the Australian husbands are also themselves recent immigrants who lack established social roots of their own. For their part, the wives, most of whom are better educated than their husbands, face the difficulties of all migrants, alone in a foreign country without the support of their families, and with the additional challenge of settling down to live with a man who is a stranger.

In a study conducted by Australia's Federal Department of Immigration and Ethnic Affairs, from a group of 40 mail-order brides in 1983, only 17 of the women had happy marriages. The study found that 'one-third of the women had no social contact, several of them being prevented or discouraged by their husbands from socialising with Filipino friends and relatives, either because the husband was anti-social or he feared the influence of other Filipinos on his wife.'

Partly because of the public concern expressed in both Australia and the Philippines about this issue, the Philippine consulate now requires Australian men to submit police clearances, proof of employment and proof that there is 'no legal impediment to marry Filipino women' and other legal documents before they will issue them with entry visas for the Philippines. The government in Manila has also announced that orientation courses will be made available to brides so that they can learn more about the culture of the countries to which they will be going.

The problem remains a serious one, not least because those who arrange the links between prospective husbands and the women not only have a financial interest in promoting the trade, but frequently remain unaccountable and engage in deception or semi-legal practices.

BRUNEI

In 1984 about 5,000 Filipinos were working in Brunei, the newest member of the Association of South East Asian Nations (ASEAN). Brunei was declared independent in January 1984 after 24 years as a British protectorate. The country is 5,765 square miles in size with a population of 200,000. It possesses large oil and gas reserves and a huge annual revenue surplus which gives its inhabitants one of the highest per capita incomes in the world (US$22,000).

Some 25,000 foreign workers run the economy — many of them Chinese residents of the country who, although they have always lived in Brunei and have no other citizenship, are considered by the government to be foreigners and do not have equal access to education, medical care or political representation. The Chinese comprise 30% of the population.[1]

Most Filipinos in Brunei are employed in the construction industry. In 1984 the Philippine and Brunei governments signed a bilateral labour agreement to establish an organised labour recruitment scheme. The agreement anticipated a growing demand for Filipino workers but since then economic growth has been cut back and it seems unlikely that the demand will be realised.

HONG KONG

The Filipino domestic workers in Hong Kong, who represent 99% of Filipinos working in the territory, have become a visible group in the community. The Sunday gatherings by Statue Square, in the heart of the business district, are one of Hong Kong's tourist sights. Hundreds of Filipinas meet there on their day off, filling the square. In a few years they have overcome immense difficulties, not least the fact that domestic workers are particularly isolated from each other. The women have succeeded in making their problems known, in securing wide coverage in the local media, and have successfully organised themselves to secure their rights under Hong Kong law and improve their social and economic status.

The first batch of domestics arrived in 1973. Their number had grown by 1980 from a few hundred to 10,000, and continued to rise sharply, to 15,000 in 1981, 19,000 in 1982, and 36,000 in 1985.[2]

This growth is linked to the economic crisis in the Philippines and the phenomenal expansion of Hong Kong's own economy. Initially, employers were mainly non-Chinese expatriates — pilots, diplomats and businessmen, who preferred English-speaking maids. But Hong Kong's rapid development as an international commercial and industrial centre has created numerous new jobs in the industrial and service sectors, which provide better paid and more independent opportunities for the young women who used to become 'amahs' (Chinese maids). As a result, experienced 'amahs' have become more expensive and the growth of Hong Kong's wealthy entrepreneurial and middle class has increased the demand for servants.

Some 80% of the Filipinas in Hong Kong are from rural communities. The majority come from northern Philippines, particularly Ilocos and the Mountain Province areas where numerous families have been dispossessed by private companies and government projects.[3] Most are young and 40% have professional skills, usually as teachers and medical workers. A very

91

'I don't usually save my money. I feel I have to spend money. I support my sisters — and what is left to me is my allowance. Hong Kong is expensive; but it is more different and more expensive in our place... What I would say to people who thought of coming to Hong Kong — realize the work you will be doing. It is different in the Philiippines because you are free...In your own country you enjoy more life, but when you stay in another country you have to work in order to live.'

high proportion are at least high school graduates or have college degrees, and therefore speak the English desired by their employer.[4]

Living and working conditions

Hong Kong is not seen by migrants as the most desirable destination. Wages are lower than those offered in the United States or Saudi Arabia. In fact, the minimum wage in Hong Kong has increased considerably, by more than 50% in real terms since 1970, although Chinese maids are paid more for fewer hours of work. In 1985, domestic workers were earning between 1,750 and 2,000 Hong Kong dollars (US$258) a month. Conditions vary widely from family to family. On the whole, it is probably true to say that most of the maids work extremely hard for a wage which is so much higher than anything they could receive in the Philippines that it partly compensates for the loneliness and monotony of their jobs.

Those who take up jobs in Hong Kong do so primarily to support members of their families back in the Philippines. Many of the teachers and educated women have despaired of earning enough to live on from the jobs which exist in their home areas. Almost all plan to return because few can marry and set up a home for themselves in Hong Kong. Because of the lack of opportunities in the Philippines, more and more are staying for as long as they can. Some have been domestics for nearly ten years.

Hong Kong government policy

It has been the policy of the Hong Kong government to permit recruitment of domestic servants from the Philippines, while ensuring that as few as possible become permanent residents of the territory. The Hong Kong authorities have acted to prevent direct abuses of recruitment procedure or maltreatment of employees by employers. But it has been made very difficult for domestics to take other kinds of employment or change their employer during the term of their two-year contracts. In addition, domestic workers are required to return to the Philippines before negotiating a new contract or renewing one which exists.

In general, the regulations are designed to benefit the employer in cases of dispute. For example, while both employers and employees may terminate contracts, a helper who does so is not free to find another job, but may be repatriated to the Philippines. She may remain only if she can both renew her visa, which is stamped for six-month periods, and secure a 'release' letter from her employer.

The 'release' letter is required before a domestic helper may apply for another job. The previous employers must affirm to the Director of Immigration that they have no objections to the helper taking a new job, and must identify the new employer. Without the employer's good will, it is obviously extremely difficult for the domestic to obtain such documentation.[5]

The Immigration Department's general policy is to refuse to license a change of job by a domestic worker during the first year of contract, and to make a change of job during the second year dependent upon the positive assent of the employer.[6]

These regulations have the effect of increasing the cost of hiring a domestic for both parties. Every two years, Filipino domestics must return to Manila and negotiate a new contract, a process during which they have to pay money to the British Embassy for new entry visas to Hong Kong, to the POEA for new papers, to the recruitment agency if they find a new employer and to the government for various exit taxes. On their side, employers have to bear the costs of air tickets, and contract fees.

More seriously, the regulations restricting the movement of workers under contract discourage them from protesting against unfair treatment by the employers. Either because they are intimidated or because they are heavily burdened by debt on their arrival and fear repatriation, many women have continued to accept considerable suffering and hardship, rather than seek families where they would be happier. In some cases, domestics have been prosecuted when they have been unable to handle their problems. One woman, for example, persuaded the daughter of her employer to sign a forged release letter when her employer terminated her contract and refused to provide her with one. The domestic was arrested and sentenced to four months imprisonment, a decision which was reversed on appeal.[7]

Inconsiderate or abusive treatment of Filipina maids is not infrequent. Like other migrants, many are defrauded by agencies in the Philippines or pay exorbitant registration fees. These are the worst forms of exploitation, and can be remedied not from Hong Kong but Manila. Cases of extortion occur in Hong Kong, nonetheless. The Independent Commission Against Corruption (ICAC) uncovered a racket in 1984, for example, in which a number of maids were made to sign over to their employers a proportion of their wages, in payment of hiring costs which were the employer's responsibility.[8]

Women have also suffered from sexual harassment or physical abuse. One domestic, hospitalised for head injuries and bruising, described her experience in a letter.

Since I start working with Mrs. P family, I had never been happy because of little mistake, she easily get mad and hurt me. I had no day off, and statutory holiday. But I was paid only Sunday, and the monthly salary,

93

excluding my statutory which she didn't pay. I start working in the morning 5:30 am and finish my work 11:30 pm. I had decided to escape last June 30 1982 because I was hit on the head by an umbrella by Mrs. P. This was not the first time she has done this thing to me.[9]

In a report published in 1983, the principal welfare organisation for Filipina domestics, the Mission for Filipino Migrant Workers, listed the problems that domestics may face: 'underpayment, non-payment of benefits and other fees, withholding of rest days and holidays, limited number of hours for rest days, being sent to work for an extra household or to work illegally for another employer, overwork, bad sleeping hours, no private sleeping quarters, not being allowed any visitors or to use the phone, always being shouted at and scolded for minor mistakes.'

In the last few years the incidence of such problems has tended to decline, largely because — perhaps more successfully than any other Filipino migrant community — the domestics in Hong Kong have been able to form organisations to represent them, and obtain the support of other voluntary associations in Hong Kong. Excellent advisory materials, covering domestic workers' rights and obligations under Hong Kong and Philippine law, have been produced by the Mission for Filipino Migrant Workers and similar organisations, and the domestics have also benefited from the free services offered by a number of lawyers. Recognising the scope for misunderstanding between employers and domestics helpers, as well as the opportunity which exists for exploitation by unscrupulous employers, the Hong Kong government acknowledges the useful services offered by many of these advisory groups, which are actively supported by the local churches.

The fact that so many Filipinas are now working in Hong Kong also means that far fewer are completely isolated from friends or sympathetic contacts.

Their sense of confidence and solidarity was demonstrated by the vigorous campaign they organised during 1984 and 1985 against the Philippine government's forced remittances policy. Under EO 857, Filipino domestics are required to remit through the banks 50% or more of their wages, and if they are unable to show proof that they have done so, the Philippine consulate refuses to provide them with travel papers. A statement and petition were supported by a public march, and by many Hong Kong associations.

The future direction of policy towards Filipino domestics in Hong Kong remains uncertain. The government has indicated that it wishes to close off entry, and eventually reduce the numbers of domestics in the territory. Many will no doubt move on to third countries, like Canada, in which a substantial number of women have already found jobs.

INDONESIA

In the 1960s and 1970s more than 7,000 Filipinos worked in Indonesia, mainly as loggers in Kalimantan. Indonesia's industrialisation programme created labour shortages in the plantations and Filipinos were among the foreign workers who filled the gap. Most left during the recession of the

Poster caricaturing the trade in brides

mid-1970s, however, and their jobs have since been filled by Indonesians. About 3,000 Filipinos now work in Indonesia, the majority in professional or supervisory posts. They represent approximately one seventh of the foreign workers officially registered in the country.[10]

95

JAPAN

Many Japanese men spend time in night clubs and cabarets, relaxing with colleagues at the end of the day. Even formal gatherings and business occasions are held in disco clubs, pubs, and cabarets, and as a result talented entertainers are in great demand. Many of them are Filipino.

Filipino artists have long held the reputation of being 'Asia's entertainers'. The penetration of Western fashions in music and dance into Japan and other Asian societies has been an advantage, since Filipinos speak English fluently and are much cheaper than Western entertainers of similar standard. They have become familiar in the entertainment centres of most major cities — Tokyo, Osaka, Yokohama, Kobe, Kyoto, Nagoya.

The majority of Filipino 'entertainers' are hostesses working clubs and bars. Commercial sex, traditionally institutionalised in Japanese society, became an industry after World War II, and is controlled by some of Japan's largest crime syndicates. The latter have organised the import of young women from the Philippines and other Southeast Asian countries to serve the legal and illegal needs of clubs, massage parlours, brothels and entertainment centres. In Japan, these imported hostesses and prostitutes have come to be called 'Japayukisan' after the young Japanese women called 'Karayukisan' who were sold by their poor families to wealthy men during and after the second world war.

Most Filipino 'Japayukisan' are neither professional singers nor accomplished dancers. Surveys have shown that they are generally young girls, aged between 16 and 23, and that the majority come from families with five or more members. A proportion are widowed or separated women, and many who become involved in the trade have very little experience of living abroad, and dream of the time when one of their Japanese customers will ask for their hand in marriage.

It is very difficult to know how many Filipino 'entertainers' are working in Japan — perhaps 20,000 — but there is general agreement that after 1982 the number of registered new contracts for entertainers fell sharply, and that Filipinos were particularly affected.[11] Agencies claim that the yearly average fell from 20,000 in 1982 to 12,000 the following year, and the All Japanese International Entertainment Promoters Federation reported that the number of Filipino contracts registered a 50% drop between 1981 and 1983.

The situation is confused, however, because it is likely that much of the fall in officially registered entertainers has been compensated by a rise in the number of Filipinas who enter the country as tourists, and then work illegally, often with the assistance of crime syndicates. These 'illegals' have even less protection from exploitation than women working in the registered entertainment industry.

This rise in the illegal immigration of women from abroad has caused the Japanese authorities to introduce stricter controls over entry and in the licensing of clubs. Incoming passengers, particularly women tourists, are screened very strictly at airports, and the government has imposed a limit on the number of entertainers which clubs and hotels may employ. In 1983 alone, 1,041 Filipinas, 557 Thais, 528 Chinese and 114 Koreans were apprehended and expelled. Of these, 68% were working as hostesses, 14% as performers of strip-tease, 4% as maids, and many of the remaining 14% as prostitutes.[12]

In some cases, Filipinas have complained of being roughly treated by the police. In November 1984, for example, *Times Journal* reported that six deported Filipinas had claimed that they had been beaten and slapped by Japanese officials when they failed to reveal the name of their Japanese recruiter.

It is unlikely that these actions have damaged the interests of those organising the trade, however, although it has probably become more difficult to secure legitimate contracts in Japan. It is relatively simple for those engaged in the pornography and prostitution business to escape legal sanctions by registering establishments which have been raided under a new name. It is legitimate to own 'massage parlours', 'love motels' and 'adult shops' in Japan, provided they are registered.

Organised prostitution in Japan is not a new phenomenon. After the Second World War, very large numbers of women became prostitutes at the American military bases in Okinawa, and during the Vietnam war Japan became — like the Philippines, Hong Kong, and Thailand — a rest-and-recreation centre for American servicemen. There are still 30,000 American servicemen in Okinawa and, as in Angeles City in the Philippines, many Filipino women work around the bases as prostitutes. It is estimated that in one area, Kin City, Filipino women even outnumber Japanese.

Conditions

Whether they are in legal or illegal work, however, the conditions which most of the hostesses and entertainers experience are difficult and exploitative.

Before leaving the Philippines, women in legitimate employment signed a contract which in 1985 set their wage at US$500 — the minimum required by the Philippine Labour Ministry. On arrival in Japan, however, they signed a second contract which set their wages rather higher (US$750 in 1985) — in accordance with the law in Japan. The second contract was fictitious. Only the first one applies, and the women were therefore paid US$250 less with the effective complicity of the Philippine authorities. Their stay in Japan began with a fraud.[13]

In practice, many of the women were paid even less than the Philippine contract stipulated, and earned no more in 1983-84 than US$250. Some were not properly paid at all. 'This is a buyers' market, and the actual working conditions are far worse than the contracts. For instance, the contract guarantees US$500-600 a month, six to eight hours of work a day, meals and one day off per week. Reality, however, is US$280-350, 10 to 12 hours a day, one day off per month, one big room for all women, and $3 to buy food they have to cook for themselves. They are allowed to take 15 minutes off while the band plays, but usually they have to work as hostesses and serve customers, so they can earn extra income.'

Their working hours usually stretch from 8 pm to 3-5am. In most cases,

97

they remain in their houses and are picked up by their employer one hour before work and accompanied home one hour after they have finished. They are given one day off per month.

There are many cases of hardship. One woman, working in Saitama Prefecture in Honjo City, lived with her employer's family; they fed and paid her so little that finally she was forced to take customers as a prostitute to make ends meet. The bachelor manager of a hotel in Tokozawa City seduced the women working for him and forced them into prostitution in his hotel. They were unable to flee because the person who formally employed them retained their passports.

MALAYSIA

Several thousand Filipinos are currently working in rubber plantations, pepper farms, logging firms and construction projects in Malaysia — where a number of Filipino women also work as domestic helpers, at a wage of about 15-20 Malaysian dollars per day.

In addition, there are some 90,000 Filipinos in Sabah in East Malaysia. Most of these people are Muslim refugees who went there during the 1970s to escape the war between Muslim secessionists and government forces in southern Philippines. They comprise one tenth of the population. The majority work in Tawau, the region's cocoa bowl, but others are employed in the timber industry and construction firms. Because they are considered to be refugees, and also entered Malaysia illegally, the status of this community is in doubt, and they are the subject of some local controversy — not least because the Philippine government has maintained a claim to sovereignty over Sabah.

PACIFIC

Filipinos can even be found in Papua New Guinea and islands in the Pacific like Samoa, where few employment opportunities might be expected to exist. Between 1979 and mid-1984 3,336 Filipino nurses and teachers took up posts in Papua New Guinea under a government to government arrangement.

SINGAPORE

After Brunei Singapore has the smallest population and the highest per capita output in the region. Bereft of natural resources, it is industrialised and has developed its own high-technology and service sectors.

The relatively high standard of living and rapid growth of the country has caused shortages of manual labour, particularly in the construction industry, although Singapore exports an average of 1,000 to 1,200 skilled workers per month.

About one-fifth of Singapore's labour force is now foreign. Filipinos account for around 15,000 (10%) of the 150,000-200,000 foreign workers in the country. Most are employed in domestic jobs, and in the construction

Dina's story

Women who work illegally are even more vulnerable. Dina first went dancing in Japan in June 1981 for US$500 a month. During that legal visit the only difficulties she faced were poor housing facilities and very late working hours. She was then only 17.

Two years later, she returned to Japan, this time on a tourist visa and under a new name. The Japanese who contacted her, whom she knew as Mr Miki, promised to pay US$650 a month for 3 months. No contract papers were signed. She was given US$325 in advance.

At the airport, she was handed US$2,500 'show money', to prove to immigration that she had money to spend. This show money was later taken away from her, and so was her return ticket.

She was housed in what she called a 'mansion' (in fact a small motel) and shared a bed with three other girls. Four other Filipino women and seven Filipino musicians were staying in the same place.

During the month she spent in Japan, Dina was transferred between four different clubs — 'Each one just as bad as the other.' The girls had to make sure that their clients drank at least 25 bottles a night.

In 'Club 229' and the 'Jump Club' in Osaka the women worked from 6 pm (and sometimes earlier) until 11 am the following morning. They did everything: they were dancers, waitresses, dish washers, cleaners, and hostesses.

They were also forced to go out with customers. For one night, each woman was paid 30,000 yen (approximately US$120), while the club received Y20,000. 'I was picked out by my employer twice, and twice I refused. On each occasion, I got slapped several times not to mention the bawlings and humiliation I got.'

The women did not talk about their problems. 'We were undergoing the same things, perhaps we were ashamed (...) The only thing we really cried aloud was our longing for home.'

After one month, the club was raided. Being an illegal worker, Dina was detained for 10 days and then deported. In the Philippines, she was contacted again by Mr Miki who paid her the US$325 balance of her salary. Why did she not file a case against him? 'I was so afraid I would read my story in the papers. Besides, there was nothing I could do. If the Philippine authorities in Japan didn't help me there, why would they now? Right now I just want to forget it all.'

Dina's sense of isolation is typical. It is certainly difficult for women in this sort of work to complain to the law. One woman who did, who refused to follow orders which were not included in her contract, and demanded her full salary, discovered the cost a few days later, when the club in which she was working was raided. She was detained and deported. She suspects her employer had a part in setting up the police raid.

and shipbuilding industries. Between 5,000 and 7,000 of the 8,000 foreign domestics in Singapore are Filipino.

Laws

Singapore's government has introduced laws regarding immigrant workers which are among the most restrictive and repressive in Asia. Foreign workers are classified either as employment pass holders, or work permit holders.

Employment passes. These are granted to workers with higher levels of skill, including university educated professionals. The creation of this category is evidence of Singapore's determination to attract the most talented and skilled people from countries in the region. Employment pass holders are subject to fewer restrictions than other workers. Their contract may by open-ended, they can marry Singaporeans, and they can bring in their families and settle permanently in the country. Their conditions of employment are relatively normal.

Work permit holders. These workers are either unskilled or considered to have less valuable skills. They are only permitted to stay for a maximum of 4 years, after which they are replaced. They are also subject to restrictions which are designed to prevent them from integrating. Some of these deny or infringe basic human rights.[14]

The phase-out plan. The Singapore government plans to phase out all work permit holders by 1991, and severely restricts the number of new contracts. At present, contracts are still granted to 'traditional sources of labour', including Hong Kong, Macao, Taiwan, South Korea, and Malaysia, on the basis that these countries provide 'high-wage, highly-skilled manpower' which matches Singapore's needs. At the end of 1982, the government announced that it would not renew work permits from countries other than Malaysia except for jobs in shipyards, construction sites and as house servants.[15]

In line with its policy, the government taxes the employment of maids. Employers used to pay a tax of 30% on foreign maids' salaries; in 1984 the tax was raised to a flat fee of S$56 (US$28) a month, in order to discourage working families from hiring foreign domestics. In 1984, one in every 10 Singaporean families in work employed a foreign maid. Despite the tax the number of foreign maids increased by 150% in the first half of the year — due, ironically, to the government's high wage policy, introduced to encourage employers to invest in labour saving technology rather than unskilled workers.[16]

Mandatory marriage permit. The most unacceptable law affecting immigrant workers is this one, which makes it illegal for a work permit holder to marry a Singaporean or a permanent resident, unless the government approves. In accordance with Singapore's immigration policy, permission to marry is only given to foreigners who have 'skills and qualifications whose absorption into the permanent workforce will be of value to the nation'. An individual who violates this racist and offensive law is subject to immediate deportation and permanently banned from returning to the country. The government has prosecuted vigorously: in 1983, 2,920 individuals were caught for this 'offence'.

Minimum wages and conditions. The Singapore government has also refused resolutely to establish any government to government agreement which would have the effect of guaranteeing minimum standards of wages and conditions for foreign workers in the country. As a result foreign workers are unprotected. In 1984 Filipina maids earned on average about S$300 per month (US$150) — roughly 15% of the average Singapore wage of S$2,000 per month (US$1,000). This differential was acknowledged by the government which declared that it wished the rate of employment of foreign workers, and wage levels, to be dictated by market forces in the private sector. With reference to domestic workers, the Minister for Labour, Mr Jayakumar, confirmed that they would continue to be excluded from the provisions of Singapore's Employment Act.

The absence of protection means that Filipina and other foreign maids are open to numerous forms of exploitation. Various additional laws and regulations further increase their vulnerability. First of all, the Singapore government requires employers to post a S$5,000 (US$2,500) Security Bond, which must be paid before he or she may hire a foreign servant. The purpose of this law, which is also deeply offensive, is to provide a guarantee that the maid will neither become pregnant nor marry in Singapore. If she does so, the employer forfeits the money. Under this policy, the maid is also required to undergo a medical check every six months.

This regulation not only denies basic rights to the women, it grants employers a moral authority to which they have no right, and encourages them to be conscious of their financial investment in their maid — indeed to treat her as a piece of insured property.

Furthermore, there are very strict controls over 'job-hopping'. A domestic helper may change employers only once every three years (and may remain in Singapore only four). She may not do so, however, unless both parties agree to the transfer and unless the rights of the maid have been abused. Whereas the maid must show proof of abuse or maltreatment, dissatisfied employers have the power to repatriate a maid at their discretion. If they do so, and file a complaint, the maid will be barred from further employment in Singapore.

The regulations covering grievances and job transfer are self-evidently biassed against the employee and protect employers from losing the money which they have paid out during the process of recruitment. The maids, in contrast, are not protected in any way from similar loss. The regulations as a whole ensure that the relationship between employer and employee is fundamentally unequal, and it is not surprising that there have been frequent cases of exploitation, abuse and sexual harassment.

Abuses

One domestic helper was forced to massage her male employer, bathe him and on one occasion to masturbate him. 'I got shocked because he suddenly stripped after telling me to massage him. I couldn't do anything because I am

101

already in his house so I massaged him. I didn't want to but he forced me. After that I bathed him in the bath tub.'[17]

The same woman was molested three times and physically abused. 'My boss caned me regularly and burned my arms with lighted cigarette.'[18] When she finally ran away her work permit was immediately cancelled. She was permitted by the immigration authorities to remain in Singapore only after a thorough investigation, and received no form of compensation.

Employers found guilty of such abuse have been imprisoned or fined. But many are not brought to justice. According to diplomats who have given refuge to runaway maids, a number of women have been sent quietly back to the Philippines after being raped by their employers. Cases of abuse also go unreported because the women are afraid they will be deported if they protest. Many have borrowed so much money to get to Singapore — up to 8,000 or 12,000 pesos (US$400-600) — that they simply cannot afford to go back

Most of the problems the maids face, however, involve non-payment or underpayment of salaries. Some girls receive only a fraction of the sums that are due to them — and some domestics have been ordered to work in their employer's factory or restaurant.

Many Filipina women have requested the Philippine Embassy to act on their behalf. But embassy officials have said that they are unable to intervene because Singapore's Employment Act does not cover maids' working conditions.

With the opening of a welfare service centre for maids by a Catholic Church in Geylang, some have been able to sort out their problems. Four lawyers provide voluntary legal service. Fr Arotcarena, the centre's head, has stated that some maids live in almost slave conditions, and the centre believes that a compulsory contract for maids, with provision for minimum wage and minimum rights, would make a lot of difference for both the maid and the employer. At present, Singapore remains one of the countries in Asia which offer the least protection or legal provision for the Filipino migrant community.

A List Of Duties And Responsibilities Drawn Up By An Employer For Her Domestic Helper In Hong Kong

I. Daily Work Schedule

6:45 a.m. — take breakfast alone
7:00 a.m. — prepare breakfast for the family
         — boil water
7:20 a.m. — dress up William for school
7:30 a.m. — feed William breakfast
7:55 a.m. — take William down to the school bus stop
8:15 a.m. — dress up Joanna and feed her breakfast
8:30 a.m. — clean the bathrooms, tidy all the bedrooms
         — sweep and mop all floors
         — wipe furnitures, clean the ceiling lights with feather brush, etc.
10:00 a.m. — get food ready for lunch, e.g. clean vegetables, defrost meat
10:30 a.m. — wash dirty clothes and hang them on line to dry
12:15 p.m. — pick up William from school and give him a change of clothes
12:45 p.m. — cook lunch
1:30 p.m. — serve lunch (have lunch yourself)
2:30 p.m. — wash the dishes
         — iron the clothes
         — take clean clothes to different rooms
5:00 p.m. — (go to the supermarket if being asked)
         — polish shoes
         — give children their baths
5:30 p.m. — make some snacks for the children (usually biscuits and milk)
         — have some snacks yourself
6:30 p.m. — prepare for dinner
8:30 p.m. — cook dinner
9:30 p.m. — serve dinner
10:00 p.m. — wash and put away dishes
         — clean the kitchen thoroughly, mop kitchen floor
         — prepare William's snack boxes

II. Things to be done every week

— change bedsheets every Sunday morning (master's bedroom and guestroom/children's bedroom alternately) — when changing sheets, sweep and mop underneath the beds
— boil all towels every Sunday
— clean inside of kitchen cupboards
— clean the lining of exhaust hood and exhaust fan in the kitchen

III. Things to be done every two weeks

— clean inside of refrigerator
— change newspaper lining on top of kitchen cupboards

IV. Things to be done once a month
— clean all the windows
— wash the bedspreads
— brush table cloth with Jiff
— polish all silverware
— clean inside of air-conditioners (only in summer)

V. Things to be done every three months
— wash curtains

VI. Conditions
— As long as you are working in this house, you have to be honest, hard-working, responsible to your duties and be very polite.
— You are requested to take your day-off on Thursday every week. You are asked to work on public holidays and will get paid the sum of HK$40.00 for the day you worked.
— You are not allowed to harm the children in any way, i.e. no spanking or hitting at any time. If the children are naughty, tell us, the parents. We will be the one to punish them.
— The washing machine is only used to wash bed sheets, big towels and bedspreads. Other clothes have to be washed by hands.
— You are not allowed to open any drawers or closets except those permitted.
— You must ask for permission to use any kind of medicine in this house.
— You are only allowed to do your personal things, e.g. writing letters, when you have finished all the work in the house.
— You are requested to have meals and snacks with the family. Try your best not to waste any food or things in the house.
— You are requested to wear your uniform during work. You can wear your own clothes on your day-offs.
— We will provide uniforms, sheets, blankets, pillow, one pair of shoes, one pair of slippers, one woolen sweater for winter. You have to take care of any other personal things you need.
— We will not allow visitation unless it is of urgent matters (seek permission first). Meet your friends on your day-offs. Phone calls to or from friends are allowed only when absolutely necessary.
— You are responsible to cook the daily meals. You will be told what dishes to cook.
— You will be asked occasionally to go to the supermarket to get a few things.
— You are not allowed to switch on the TV or the Hi-fi system or airconditioners unless with permission.
— If you are not satisfied with working in this house, you have to give a one month's notice before you can quit. If we are not happy with your work, we can send you back to the Philippines right away according to the contract.

9. SEAFARERS

'To be a "good" Filipino is to remain silent.'

A Filipino third mate.

Filipino seafarers — who numbered over 54,000 in 1984, crewing ships registered in 69 different countries — lead lives very different from other groups of migrant workers. At sea for most of their working lives, they live in very disciplined, small, mostly male communities, isolated from wider society and often only staying in ports for eight hours before setting sail again.

While the vast majority of Filipino seafarers work on cargo ships (container ships, bulk carriers and tankers) an increasing percentage work on some of the 160 luxury cruise ships which serve the world's tourist industry. Working hours on cruise ships are often very long — up to 100 a week. Crew living quarters are cramped and recreational opportunities very limited since the crew are not usually allowed to fraternise with passengers. Fines are arbitrarily imposed on seafarers who wander into passenger areas without a reason. And depending on the routes followed by the ship, opportunities to go ashore even for an hour are limited. For example, a kitchen worker on a Carnival Line ship which leaves from Miami once or twice a week must work both sittings of three meals every day plus the midnight buffet three or four days of the week. Free time, even to make a phone call, is limited. Weeks can go by without shore leave.

On cargo ships there is far more crew living space than on cruise ships and there is not the same pressure of serving the public, but the working hours can be very long. Only a few cargo ships have recreation facilities like table tennis, let alone the gymnasiums or swimming pools that may be found on the most modern vessels. There may be a smoking or recreation room with T.V. and video. Most sailors spend their hours off-duty in the mess room, where they can talk, drink beer or coffee and play chess. The sailors don't read many books but love comics, which they sometimes receive from a chaplain/ship visitor and exchange between themselves. When crews are of mixed nationality, relations are sometimes difficult, particularly during long voyages. In general, however, Filipinos have a reputation for being relaxed and relatively easy to get on with.

Of the 54,000 Filipino active seafarers working in international shipping, 4,892 work on ships registered in the Philippines. Of the balance, 38,000 (70%) work on flag of convenience ships. These are ships which are registered in countries different from the country where the ship is owned. Thus the owners are able to save on taxes and on crew costs. Over half of all Philippine seamen work on the ships of just two flag of convenience countries, Panama (20,024) and Liberia (12,130).

26% of all Filipino seafarers work as officers but only 1% are captains; 42% are senior ratings (experienced and qualified workers). The rest hold entry positions on the deck, in the kitchen and in the engine room.

Filipino seafarers are often preferred to workers from other labour exporting countries — South Korea and Taiwan for example — because they speak English and are known as cooperative and hard working.

Nevertheless, unemployment in the industry is growing.

The international shipping industry grew very rapidly during the oil boom of the late 1970s, but suffered a deep depression in the 1980s. Several of the largest shipowners have gone bankrupt, while others have been forced to cut costs in every way possible. The easiest way is to cut wages since it is often impossible to economise on wharfage fees and other fixed operating costs.

There are as many as 200,000 unemployed Filipino seafarers waiting in line for jobs. The pool of unemployed is partly so large because maritime training schools have proliferated in recent years. It is said that there are 54 nautical schools in the Philippines, graduating as many as 10,000 students each year, all looking for jobs in international shipping. But the number of jobs has fallen from 64,150 in 1982 to 54,000 in 1984. Experienced Filipino seafarers resent the large number of schools, some of which do not maintain the quality of training for which the Philippines was once famous.

Several of the crew-exporting countries are in competition with each other to provide well-trained crews. At the present time the Philippines has agreed to abide by the minimum standard wage suggested by the International Labour Office (ILO) in Geneva. In 1984 this was US$276.00 per month for a qualified deck hand. But this policy is threatened by countries such as Bangladesh, which is sending seafarers abroad for as little as US$120.00 a month. The Philippine authorities are tempted to find ways to cut salaries in order to keep jobs.

Filipino seafarers are caught in the squeeze. The People's Republic of China is currently training seafarers and is already placing some on foreign flag ships. If China follows an aggressive policy, and offers qualified Chinese seafarers at US$50 a month, there is a serious question about what would happen to Filipino jobs.

The training maze

Traditionally there are two ways to launch a maritime career. Deckhands, kitchen and engine room workers are generally hired as apprentices. Entry level seafarers working on the deck are called ordinary seamen (OS). They do all the routine chores required to maintain a ship constantly threatened by salt water rust. With experience these seafarers are promoted to the rank of able-bodied seaman (AB), which requires a knowledge of rope and cargo handling and deck machinery. ABs also serve watches at the helm under the direction of the navigating officer.

The other way of starting a maritime career, besides apprenticeship, is to attend maritime school. After three or four years of schooling, candidates for deck or engine room officers are normally required to spend a year as an officer apprentice. In the Philippines this experience is gained usually in the domestic inter-island shipping fleet. In former times an officer apprentice received a salary like any other shipboard worker. But today it is difficult to find a job to get qualifying experience, and apprentices sometimes pay the ship owner for the privilege of working on board and even for their keep.

To get a seaman's book — an external document — it has become necessary to pass through one of the many nautical training and re-training

107

The problems of a seafarer

'Alonso is a twenty-seven-year-old Filipino seafarer, a native of Cebu. He first went to sea six years ago and served his apprenticeship working for a Chinese-owned company based in Mindanao. He was an engine room apprentice on a small ship carrying logs and bananas up and down the coast. He had to pay the company just to be taken in as an apprentice.

When he first started shipping international he was far more satisfied than today. He was paid more money then, allotments were sent to his home quicker. He is now increasingly unhappy with this work, and is finding it more and more difficult to find a job.

At the hands of his own Filipino government he feels he suffers constant harassment. Having already graduated from one of the country's 54 maritime training schools, he has just now been required to contact one of the twenty-six newly created re-training centres. But there was no re-training! He simply had to pay 1200 pesos ($70.00) for a new certificate. And to receive re-endorsement from the Philippine Coast Guard, he had to pay off the examiners.

To actually find a job — his last company went bankrupt — he must first obtain a valid Seaman's Registration Card (SRC) from the Philippine Overseas Employment Administration (POEA) as proof that he is registered with the manpower pool. Then he must go to one of the 200 manning agents now licensed by the POEA; and to hurry this application along he has to pay almost $500 in fees. Even then he has to wait several months. (The 'stand-by' period is now from three to fifteen months.) In June, 1983, he signed a contract with the Maybeh Shipping Services, Inc. as a Third Assistant Engineer on a ship which he would meet in Durban, RSA. Contrary to standard maritime custom, the cost of the plane ticket, which was bought by the manning agent, is being deducted from his monthly salary.

The contract which he signed with Maybeh had some unsettling paragraphs: 'It is fully agreed that seamen who are signatory under this contract shall not in any manner voluntarily or otherwise enter into any bargaining or affiliation with any organization such as ITF or any seaman's union.' The problem with this is that under the laws of Panama, as in the Human Rights documents of the United Nations, to which the Philippines is a signatory, there is an unviolable right to join a labour union. Alonso is hesitant to sacrifice this basic right.

'It is further agreed that any officer or crew member who in one way or another affiliates or joins such organizations as mentioned above and causes the vessel and owners financial losses or delay to the vessel, such officer/crew member shall be made liable to the owner/ agent answerable in the court of laws for the recovery of such amounts that have been received over and above their contracted and POEA

Seafarers

approved and verified valid contract. Owners/agents reserve the rights to sue for any other damages/losses that may be incurred by the owners and agents in connection to such affiliation.

'That it is further agreed that any amount of money received, that which is over and above the POEA verified contract shall only be held in trust by crew members or allottee and that it shall be returned to the Master by crew members and/or allottee to agents in case it has reached allottee.

'That we the undersigned, recognize the fact that failure to return the money will constitute "estafa" (fraud). We finally declare that I/We are signing this addendum to our contract in and of our own free will and voluntarily.' The experience of many Filipino seafarers who have amicably settled disputes abroad, only to have the case reopened by the agents when the seafarers return to the Philippines, are too well known to Alonso. He has friends who are unable to find any jobs because years ago their ships were involved with ITF actions. Here's how it happens: The Filipino Association for Mariners' Employment (FAME) maintains a list of those involved in ITF actions. If your name is on that list the chance of processing your employment contract is frozen.

When Alonso finally reached the ship in Durban in late June 1983, he was told that they had no need for a Third Assistant Engineer; the only job available was for an oiler. 'Take it or leave it.' And what about the contract he signed in the Philippines? The Master knew nothing about it. At the rate of pay he was being offered as an oiler — $230 a month, including fixed overtime — he will have to work months before he even pays back the money which he borrowed to get the job. But what choice does he have? He has no money for the return air fare, and no assurance that he will find another job. There are four unemployed Filipino seafarers waiting for each available job.

He reluctantly signed on to this sub-standard ship, which was dirty, with a hostile atmosphere, with 16-hour work days and no days off.

Finances were complicated by allotment payments. He at first received his $46.00 monthly wage (20% of his wages). But letters from his wife indicated that she was not receiving her allotments. He complained to the captain, who said it was not his fault. The money was being sent by the company to the manning agent who reportedly was depositing the money in the bank account of the allottee, which in this case is Alonso's wife. There must be an administrative hang-up. Now Alonso has been writing to the Panamanian Consulate, to the owner, and to his manning agent without success, seeking both a refund for his ticket to Durban, and an investigation of his allotment troubles. He doesn't know anywhere else to turn.'

From: *Ang Timon* — newspaper for Filipino Seafarers 1985

schools. Many of these do little more than issue a required certificate — for a fee, of course. Even qualified officers, including the Master and the Chief Engineer, must submit to retraining on a regular basis. In an industry which is increasingly sophisticated, technical retraining is theoretically desirable. But in practice, experienced officers say that they are humiliated by the simplistic courses in fire fighting, radar, life boat and ARPA (Advanced Radar Plotting Aids) which they must go through in order to receive their retraining certificates. Officers refer to these courses as 'electronic games'. Because of serious corruption in European and American manning agencies in the early decades of the 20th century one of the first actions of the International Labour Office (ILO) was to try to clear up manning irregularities. In 1920 the ILO passed Convention 9, which was soon ratified by many maritime nations, stating that it was illegal for anyone to profit from the placing of a seafarer. It is likewise against the law in the Philippines. But the law is scandalously ignored.

Not only nautical schools seek to profit from the seafarers' labour. There are 200 or more employment agencies also making a living from the seafarer. Filipino employment agencies are licensed by the Philippine Overseas Employment Agency (POEA) which has the authority to rescind licences, and occasionally does so. But it is difficult to prove an illegal payment has taken place. The seafarers generally want a job more than they want to punish the abusers.

Every seafarer knows that the Filipino Association of Mariners' Employment (FAME) maintains what they call the 'black' list of seafarers who make trouble. No one has seen it or knows exactly what must be done to get on it, but it means you will probably never get a job again. If you haven't been paid for six months and you complain to the POEA and they launch an investigation, will your name appear on the FAME list? No seafarer can be sure, and so to preserve job prospects Filipino seafarers often suffer the indignity of exploitation rather than stand up for their rights. They remain hostage to the extremely high unemployment rate. As one Third Mate said recently, 'To be a good Filipino is to remain silent.'

Before taking a job a seafarer is required to participate in pre-departure briefings which include warnings about making trouble once aboard ship. And the POEA maintains representatives in overseas ports, ostensibly to allow inspection of ships, but in reality to ensure that seafarers conform to POEA policies. Some seafarers must sign undertakings to the effect that they will not cause 'trouble', as in the case of Alonso Esquino, quoted above.

Employment problems

On October 28 1985, four highly qualified Filipino musicians walked off the ship on which they had been working for two weeks. They had been the victims of a fraudulent scheme perpetrated by a Manila-based maritime employment agency called Liberty Marine.

The men were told by agents of Liberty Marine that they would be hired as musicians on the *Bermuda Star*, a Panamanian luxury cruise ship which sails

Paying to work

'Felix has worked on a one-year contract on three different ships of the Oster Lines. His record is excellent. One engineering officer has written a recommendation saying that Felix does the work of three people. He is cooperative, sober, and industrious.

When Felix left his last ship, the *Ariadne*, in 1981, he was told by the Manila manning agent that after his normal one-month vacation (without pay), he would have to pay $600 to get another job with the same company. Felix has refused on the grounds that he is a regular and dependable employee of Oster and that he doesn't believe he should make an illegal payment. Meanwhile less qualified seafarers who are willing to pay the price are being employed by Oster and Felix remains unemployed.'

from New York to Bermuda in the summer months, and from New Orleans to the Caribbean in the winter. They were promised a very favourable contract, with good conditions and a salary of $800.00 a month. They were also assured that they would be accommodated in passenger quarters on the ship and one man, a vegetarian, was told he could prepare his own food.

The manning agency invented a new name for the group — 'The Polytones' — and asked them to sign a 'dummy' contract, ostensibly for employment on the *Noordam*, a cruise ship operated on the West Coast of the United States by the Holland America Line. The musicians were told that signing this contract would facilitate visa procedures, but that a true contract reflecting employment on the *Bermuda Star* would be furnished when they arrived in New York. They were then given an advance on their first month's salary. At the same time they were each charged a US$250.00 manning agency fee.

When they arrived in New York the ship was in Bermuda, and after many inconveniences and rebuffs they were finally flown to Bermuda to meet the ship. They were taken to cabins which were not anything like the passenger cabins they had been shown, but were filthy and stank. When they complained they were then given cabins below the water line, next to the engine room. They immediately asked the cruise director about their contract. He indicated that it would not be forthcoming. So they asked to be repatriated. But that request was also refused. In effect, they were given no chance.

The work schedule to which the men were submitted absolutely exhausted them. The day they arrived, from halfway around the world, they had to rehearse from midnight until after 5.00 am. Though one of the musicians was desperately seasick, they had to perform while sailing through Hurricane Gloria. The vegetarian was not allowed to prepare his own food.

They again protested to the ship's authorities and said unless they received a contract guaranteeing their rights, they wanted to be returned to the Philippines. They were told to be patient, in another week the situation would improve and they would have a contract.

111

Seafarers' demonstration, Manila

This week went by, and conditions did not improve. And there was no contract. The men began to realise that they were victims of a fraudulent deception perpetrated by the manning agency and the ship owner. The ship had no intention of delivering what had been promised. So one hour before the ship was due to sail from New York on September 28, 1985, they walked off, leaving most of their luggage behind.

This malpractice is technically called 'contract substitution', and Filipino seafarers are victimised by it far too often. They sign one contract, or even blank contract papers in the manning agent's office. But when they sign ship's articles, the conditions they expected are not honoured and they must settle for less. A copy of the true contract is on file at the POEA and an aggrieved seafarer who wants to know what the manning agent intends as his conditions on board may contact the POEA for this information. But it is not easy for a Filipino seafarer on the high seas to contact the POEA.

Some seafarers have been caught in the middle of a dispute between the International Transport Workers' Federation (ITF) and the shipowners. ITF, a London-based federation of maritime and other unions, has fought against the flag of convenience phenomenon by seeking to negotiate contracts for seafarers which will stop the deterioration of wages and working conditions. ITF rates are approximately two and a half times higher than ILO rates, and naturally Filipino seafarers are eager for this increase.

The ITF campaign works like this; when a flag of convenience ship arrives in a port where ITF unions are active, such as Australia, the local union can hold up the ship until an ITF contract is signed.

To deceive ITF inspectors, some ships maintain two sets of accounts. One shows that ITF wages are being paid, and this set is produced when the ship enters ITF-controlled ports. The other set of books shows the real wage situation.

In some cases, seafarers have received ITF wages in a port and have then been required to refund the money once the ship has sailed again.

One case heard by the Supreme Court of the Philippines illustrates the conflicts which seafarers may face. Seafarers in December 1978 and January 1979 signed contracts with Virjen Shipping and Marine Services to work on the *M/t Jannus*, a ship normally trading in the Caribbean. The contracts were duly approved. But after signing the contract the captain was informed by the ship's managers that the vessel was to proceed to Australia, where ITF inspectors would be expected to board. The company then changed the terms of the contract and ostensibly enrolled the seamen in the ITF, to avoid problems in Australia. They never intended to pay ITF wages, but this was their ploy to avoid ITF interdiction in Australia.

In view of the fact that the company had already broken their contract, the crew subsequently petitioned for a 50% increase in their basic wages. The company in reply proposed a 25% increase, which the seamen accepted, but when they reached Japan again on April 19 they were all sacked and repatriated to the Philippines, only three months into their 12-month contract.

Executive Order 857 presented another problem. It required sailors to remit 80% of their wage in Western currency through the ship's manager to the manning agency which had employed them. The money was deposited in an authorised bank and credited to the account of a designated allottee — a spouse, parent, or relative. In 1984, over US$200 million dollars flowed into the Philippine banks from the seafarers. Although they constitute only 15% of the overseas work force, seafarers' earnings supplied 30% of the foreign exchange remittances credited by the POEA.

Delays in the payment and clearance of remittances are not uncommon. Many Filipino seafarers receive letters from their families months after they have been working on the seas, saying that the first remittance has not yet cleared the banking system. Delays can range from one to as many as 10 months. This puts a great strain on the families who depend on this support and on the seafarer, who feels powerless to do anything on behalf of his loved ones.

In addition, the Filipino seafarer sending his remittances through official banking channels also feels cheated, as the official exchange rate of dollars to Philippine pesos is generally lower than the 'black market' exchange rate.

Traditionally, ship owners are responsible for providing adequate health care on their vessels. Merchant ships are not required to carry doctors, but at least one of the officers (usually the First Mate) must have a minimum knowledge of basic medicine and the ship has to be equipped with basic

113

medical supplies. Radio contact with medical experts is usually available. A sick or injured seafarer must be given the best treatment available while at sea, and when the ship reaches port the company is responsible for providing medical care usually for up to 30 weeks. In the case of permanent injury the seafarer is often entitled to an indemnity.

Such rights are not always easy to sustain in practice and Filipino seafarers have often had to hire a lawyer to protect themselves.

Benito had been working in the engine room for eight months when one day he fell while walking down the greasy companionway and broke his arm, quite severely. The Chief Mate did put a splint on it and when they arrived in port nine days later the agent took Benito to a local osteopathic surgeon to see what more should be done. The surgeon said that further surgery would be required to reset the arm. That night a private security guard came to the ship and took Benito to the airport to be repatriated. The company thus has tried to avoid the cost of his treatment. So far Benito has been unsuccessful in contacting the owner to pay for the operation which was required.

The right to leave the employ of a ship is inviolable. Ships are not prisons. Seafarers in the past could be imprisoned for desertion, but today they have the right to cut short their contract. However, there will probably be penalties for doing so. Among these is the sacrifice of repatriation expense. Normally at the end of a contract the shipping company will pay the cost of transportation home. (In the same way it is usually the responsiblity of the company to pay the transportation from the Philippines to meet the ship wherever it is). But if the worker leaves prematurely the worker must bear the cost of return transportation, and sometimes is responsible for the cost of the transportation for a replacement worker.

114

Unions

Filipino seafarers are not highly organised, and those unions which do exist do not have a good record of acting effectively on behalf of their members. Union membership becomes necessary only if a sailor gets a job through one of the many agencies which are described as belonging to the 'Captain Oca' group; these include Walem, C.F. Sharp, and NAESS, among others. The union associated with these agencies is the Associated Marine Officers' and Seamen's Union of the Philippines (AMOSUP), which is affiliated to the Philippine Transport and General Workers' Union headed by Captain Gregorio Oca, brother of the former Assemblyman Oca. PTGWU is the Philippine affiliate of the ITF. The union therefore signs ITF agreements with ship owners. Unfortunately the agencies with which Oca is associated have been among those which have required seamen to sign a second contract, stipulating inferior salaries and conditions.

The right of Filipino seafarers to strike is very limited. The seafarers' claim may also fall between several conflicting legal authorities. The Philippines claims to have jurisdiction in law over cases concerning its nationals. The country in which the ship is registered claims jurisdiction over all internal matters on its ships and in certain cases the port state may also claim its laws take precedence.

The right to strike is guaranteed under the terms of the Universal Declaration of Human Rights, and by the laws of flag-of-convenience countries such as Liberia, Panama and the Bahamas, though limitations are prescribed to assure the safety of the ship. This right is often not realised in practice, however, since Filipino seafarers fear that if they strike they may face reprisals, or jeopardise future job opportunities.

In the United States, where a foreign seafarer has the right to receive his contract wages, the US courts will take action to support the claims of seafarers who have not been paid. It is the responsiblity of the ship's

115

managers to prove that they have paid the wages and, if they cannot do so, courts will seize the ship and if necessary sell it to get the money that the seafarer is due. The Centre for Seafarers' Rights in the US provides free legal help to seafarers who have not been paid.

In other countries, lawyers can also help crews to put a lien on a ship and prevent it leaving port until wages have been paid.

Seafarers in port

A lot of seafarers do not go ashore at all because the time in port is too short. A modern container ship or tanker can offload very rapidly — 4,000 cars, for example, can be driven off a car carrier in five hours. Seafarers, who may have spent 25 days at sea travelling from Japan to the East Coast of the US, may not even have an opportunity to make a phone call, if the port call falls during working hours. Bulk carriers and general cargo ships, on the other hand, may often spend two or three days in port, offloading, allowing opportunities for some shore visits (in countries which allow seafarers to disembark).

For those seafarers who do have an opportunity to go ashore, in 600 ports around the world there are church-based 'Seamen's Centres', often located near port facilities. The chaplains, who are linked together through an organisation called The International Christian Maritime Association, can be of great help to Filipino seafarers. Most give good advice — all can offer a welcome, help to send mail or make phone calls, and perhaps arrange a tour of the port city or a shopping tour if there is time. Occasionally in some of these Centres the chaplains put pressure on the seafarers to 'convert' to a particular Christian group, but this practice is increasingly rare.

PART 3
THE ECONOMIC COSTS

10. THE MACRO-ECONOMIC EFFECTS OF LABOUR MIGRATION – AN OVERVIEW

'Overseas employment addresses two major problems: unemployment and the balance of payments position.'
Ferdinand Marcos, 1982

It is generally believed that international labour migration has positive effects on the economies of capital-rich labour-importing countries. Since the Second World War, and particularly when their economies are in rapid expansion, all advanced capitalist countries have imported labour — as have the newly industrializing oil-rich countries in the Gulf region, and financial and trading centres such as Hong Kong and Singapore. Employers are continuously searching for flexible labour units. Temporary foreign workers are particularly valuable, because they provide labour as and where required, without inflationary effects on the host countries' wages or social expenditure, and can be sent back to their own countries as soon as they are no longer needed.[1]

It is not so clear, however, that this exchange, so beneficial to the developed economies, is really to the long-term advantage of labour-exporting countries. Proponents of the Philippine government's manpower export policy have argued vigorously that selling human labour, like any other commodity in the world market, is economically and socially beneficial. They argue that manpower export earns foreign exchange which provides immediate, albeit temporary, relief to balance of payments problems, creates jobs, thereby alleviating local unemployment, and provides opportunities for workers to acquire new skills.

As early as 1976 President Marcos asserted that through the overseas employment promotion programme:

We have provided jobs for our people not only in our new and expanding industries but also in the world labor market. Filipino talents and skills are becoming ubiquitous in many parts of the world. Returning Filipino workers have helped improve our skills and technological standards.

And in 1982 he reaffirmed:

For us, overseas employment addresses two major problems: unemployment and the balance of payments position. If these problems are met or at least partially solved by contract migration, we also expect an increase in national savings and investment levels. In the long run, we also expect that overseas employment will contribute to the acquisition of skills essential to the development of the country's industrial base.[2]

The foreign exchange argument
There has been a tremendous increase in foreign exchange remittances by Filipino overseas workers since 1976. Between 1976 and 1983, receipts increased by more than 500%, from US$158.4mn to US$955mn. By 1979 remittances were the second highest source of foreign currency — ahead of

copper, logging, electronics exports, sugar and textiles. In addition, the large incomes of overseas workers increased government receipts from income taxes.

It is argued that the large expendable incomes which workers remit to their families in the Philippines will be spent not only on consumption but also on local productive investment and capital formation. Increased spending in the local economy will generate demand for local products, thereby encouraging the growth of local trade, and in time increase by the 'multiplier effect' the country's productive capacity and Gross National Product (GNP). At the individual level, workers' families will become prosperous, while the government will benefit from increased tax receipts and from larger reserves of foreign currency which are necessary to fund development projects.

These assumptions are challenged on several grounds. There is, first of all, a sizeable gap between the real earnings of overseas workers and the amount which they actually remit through the banking system. According to Central Bank estimates, this gap amounted in 1981 to US$290.37mn — or well over 50% of the US$525.43mn in remittances which were recorded, indicating a leak in the system. It is impossible to know what happens to the money which flows in through the Philippine black market but it clearly means a loss in tax revenues.

Nor, at least during the presidency of Ferdinand Marcos, is the record of government spending a reassuring one. Independent studies suggest most of the dollar inflows were spent on the import of oil and a wide range of consumer goods, on large and wasteful infrastructural projects, and on servicing the interest charges on the country's huge foreign debt of at least US$26 billion (1985).[3]

A report by a panel of economists at the University of the Philippines commented, for example, that:

The bulk of construction and other capital outlay in both the private and public sectors were not very productive and many were outrightly wasteful... In many instances, though the outward purpose of projects might be endowed with some plausible economic or social justification, a more urgent reason for pursuing them was the opportunity to use government activity as a vehicle for private gain, whether pecuniary or political. Examples would be overdesigned bridges, highways, public buildings or large energy projects designed to secure a political constituency, to get a commission, or to corner a contract.[4]

Business Day reported in 1984 that 52% of the country's total foreign exchange earnings would be spent on repaying principal to the World Bank and the International Monetary Fund (IMF), and US$2.4bn in interest payments to about 300 foreign private banks.[5]

If the Philippine government has failed to use workers' remittances to fund the long-term development of the country, are the overseas workers

121

themselves, and their families, in a better position to invest their savings productively?

A university study on the families of migrant workers indicated that 'very few households use remittances on productive investment'.[6] In order of priority, remittances are spent on: 1) basic necessities; 2) debt repayment; 3) education of children; 4) housing needs. Savings lie fifth in the order of priority. This pattern of spending — concentrated heavily on subsistence and consumption — has been confirmed in other countries and by other studies of the Philippines including the government's Overseas Employment Development Board (OEDB).

Only a very small percentage of migrants were able to start new businesses as a result of their work overseas. The De La Salle University report found that no more than 4% were able to do so and further concluded that there was little prospect of change in the short term.

> Investment possibilities in the home country are culturally defined, economically circumscribed and subject to political filters. The very factors that push workers into emigrating will be the same factors that will frustrate the migrants' or their families' domestic investment efforts.[7]

The nature of remittances accounts for their unreliability as a long-term source of foreign exchange to fuel the country's economic development — a point emphasised by the remarks of a senior official of the POEA:

> Remittances take an inverted U pattern, small in the beginning, gets increasingly higher, peaks, then declines. The amount and proportion of income remitted varies directly with the strength of social and economic ties to the home country and inversely with how well the migrants are established in the host country.'[8]

The government has made great efforts to promote overseas employment. Its aim in doing so was to generate foreign exchange. In this, for at least a period during the 1970s and early 1980s, it was successful. However, there has never been any prospect that the country's poverty or economic crisis can be solved by this means. The haemorrhage of national wealth which is due to the country's unequal trade relations, open-door trade policy and dependence on foreign loans, can never be replaced by the private thrift of overseas workers — however numerous they become.

The employment argument

In 1983 the Philippine workforce numbered about 20.5 million, out of a total population of 52 million according to official figures. Of these 1.2 million were declared unemployed, and 5.8 million were classed as underemployed. According to other economists these figures understate the level of unemployment, which may affect more than one third of the workforce.

Since the mid-1970s the Philippines has exported more than 1.5 million workers. It is argued that the overseas employment strategy benefits the country by providing work for a proportion of the unemployed and reducing the cost to the local economy of supporting this great multitude.[9] The Institute of Labour and Manpower Studies (ILMS) estimated that to 'absorb 167,000 workers (the number of workers that migrated from 1972 to 1976) into domestic employment would require anything from P1.8bn to P29bn (US$150m — 2.4bn at US$1 to P12) in investments depending on the industry that employs them.'[10]

Table 4: Processed Overseas Contract Workers, 1975-83

Year	Landbased	Seabased	Total
1975	12,501	23,534	36,035
1976	19,221	28,614	47,835
1977	36,676	33,699	70,375
1978	50,961	37,280	88,241
1979	92,519	44,818	137,337
1980	157,394	57,196	214,590
1981	210,936	55,307	266,243
1982	250,115	64,169	314,284
1983	380,263	53,944	434,207
			1,609,147

Source: Philippine Overseas Employment Administration 1983 Annual Report.

As the White Paper on Overseas Employment points out, however:

It is essentially the better skilled and qualified among the members of the segments of the labor market who are employed abroad. These are usually people who already have jobs or do not find it difficult to find one. Once they are siphoned off by the overseas market, others who are less qualified or who possess less training and experience fill in the vacancies left.(...) By implication, the overseas employment program contributes only indirectly to the alleviation of the economy's unemployment problem.

This conclusion is supported by the government's own statistics on the employment status of contract workers prior to their stint abroad (see Table 5).

Only 17% of overseas contract workers had no working experience before they went abroad. The figures confirm that the migrants tend to be drawn from the more experienced and qualified workers in the prime of their working lives. This is not surprising — foreign employers come to the Philippines precisely to recruit such people. It is not surplus labour which is being sent abroad but the best among the employed.

It is also worth emphasizing that a considerable number of migrants take second or third contracts, suggesting that the real uptake of unemployed workers may be much lower than the figures suggest — and that many of the

123

Table 5: Work Experience of Overseas Contract Workers

Years of Work	Number	Percentage
None	136	17.0
1-2 years	130	16.2
3-5 years	184	23.0
6-10 years	175	22.0
11-15 years	78	9.7
16-20 years	65	8.1
21 years or more	32	4.0
Total	800	100.0

Source: ILMS, Socio-Economic Consequences of Contract Labor Migration in the Philippines, Vol. II, p. 52.

skilled workers who go abroad do not return to the Philippines for a number of years. Many may live away for most of their working lives. In 1983 for example, there were 143,010 rehires out of 434,207 contracts — almost exactly one-third.[11] If the trend is confirmed it will further reduce the impact of overseas employment on domestic unemployment, because many of the overseas workers will simply be circulating in the overseas market. The position of Philippine migrant workers is likely in any case to be much weaker in the future. The demand for migrant labour internationally has dramatically contracted in recent years, in particular in the Middle East as a result of falling oil prices and an end to massive state capital projects. Thus, overall there will be fewer and fewer opportunities for new entrants.

The very same statistics used to justify the claim that overseas employment alleviates local employment problems, can also prove the opposite point.

The official unemployment figures between 1978 and 1983 are not encouraging. As a proportion of the labour force the rate of unemployment increased from 5.2% to 5.9% over the period: those out of work rose from 0.8 to 1.2 million. Underemployment grew even faster from 10.2% to 29.0 % of labour: the number of underemployed people rose from 1.6 million in 1976 to 5.8 million in 1983. Among these, the 'visibly underemployed' (those working less than 64 days per quarter, who want additional work) increased from 0.7 million to 2.2 million. Though many causes underlie the soaring underemployment and the general economic crisis of the Philippine economy which became apparent during this period, it is clear that the government's manpower export programme has not solved the unemployment problem.

In fact, labour migration does not benefit those people most in need of employment. The demand overseas is for professionals and skilled or semi-skilled workers. As a result, few agricultural and unskilled workers who compose the majority of the population and of the unemployed are able to find work abroad.

A graduate class in Public Administration at the University of the Philippines (U.P.) also found that access to recruitment centres and information was biased in favour of urban areas. They wrote:

124

The overseas employment program provides services limited to areas within or near the city property where MOLE branches are located and which can facilitate recruitment and hiring of workers for overseas employment and not in the so-called 'more depressed' sectors of the country which are found mostly in the far-flung areas.

It is true that the manpower export programme has brought comparative prosperity and relatively better job opportunities to many individual Filipinos. The De La Salle report shows that almost all migrants' families feel they gain in personal economic terms. But the long-term advantages to the community are far more doubtful, and when the demand for international contract labour declines, the future will become very uncertain. To absorb all returning migrant workers into the local economy and new workers who enter the labour market (which has been growing annually by 3.4%) the government would need to create 3.7 million more jobs between 1985 and 1990. According to the (now defunct) BES this would require a GNP growth rate of 8% a year. [12] It is currently assumed that the Philippine economy will still be growing very slowly even at the end of this decade.

The 'savings on capital' advertised by the government can offer no more than a temporary respite, at best, to inevitable expenditure in the future. Eventually, the government has to face the formidable tasks of providing productive work for the country's growing population, including the returning migrants.

Finally, recent research suggests that the migrant labour system may have worsened the already unequal distribution of wealth. The U.P. report says about this aspect of the question that

Estimates based on National Census and Statistics Office (NCSO) 1971 family income and expenditure survey and the 1979 integrated survey of households (ISH) show that the income distribution worsened between 1971 and 1979. The poorest 60% of total households, which received only 25.0% of total income in 1971, suffered a further decline of their share to 22.5 percent in 1979 while the richest 10 percent of households increased their share of total income from 37.1 percent in 1971 to 41.7 percent in 1979. [13]

Skill drain and de-skilling

Replacing the skills lost abroad due to labour migration is an expense to the national economy. The majority of migrant workers are skilled and semi-skilled (78 %) and a large proportion of the remainder are professionals and managers. Migrants are highly literate. Almost eight out of every 10 finished secondary education, 36% have a degree and another 13% studied at college. The majority of workers also had some years of work experience prior to going abroad. [14]

When he was Minister of Labor, Mr Blas Ople deplored the skill drain which had taken place in some Philippine firms. He cited the case of a local oil company which lost every one of its top operators to overseas employers and was obliged to reduce output for several months. Another local power company was forced to staff many of its stations with trainees, a situation which led to power failures in Luzon and Manila. Mr Placido Mapa, Economic Planning Minister under President Marcos, has also pointed out that 'the Philippine industrialization drive, as envisioned in the country's five-year plan, may suffer' due to lack of trained manpower.[15]

The temporary migration of agricultural engineers, for example, may be beneficial to the workers concerned, but may set back irrigation in a whole province, with numerous knock-on effects on the local economy. These are costs which are not reflected in the rate-of-return calculation, but are just as important to the well-being of society.

The loss of important skills through temporary migration is difficult to replace and may also cause considerable damage by slowing down production. Certain skills take time to acquire, and are expensive to teach. This cost of large-scale migration is beginning to be felt by the local business sector. The Employers Confederation of the Philippines requested the government to establish a Training Fund

> for the exclusive purpose of funding the manpower training programs of the National Manpower and Youth Council (NMYC), Construction Development Manpower Foundation and other industry boards. Such training fund will be levied on employers except those who have duly accredited training programs and those who send their own employees abroad.[16]

According to *Business Day*, in 1980 there were labour shortages in numerous critical industries including petro-chemicals, tele-communications, aviation, power, hotels (skilled workers), and agricultural research and technology.[17] Representatives of some industries formally expressed their fears that the movement abroad of technical staff would cause shortages of trained personnel: they included the Philippine Association of Flour Millers Inc. (PAFMI), the Bus Operators' Association of the Philippines (BOAP) and the Philippine Contractors' Association.[18] Patricia Santo Tomas, who is now Administrator of the POEA, has also declared in the past that 'the local supply of skills may be dwindling at a rate that is proportionately larger than the rate of replacement.'[19]

A recent and detailed study conducted by the Institute of Industrial Relations of the University of the Philippines found that:

> The ratio of foreign demand to the number of new entrants to the labor force is quite alarming in certain skill categories. For service workers, for instance, the number employed abroad exceeds the number entering the local market. The highest ratio recorded was 704.5 per cent (1979). Likewise, the outflow of production workers was higher than the number of new entrants in 1977, 1981 and 1982. On the other hand, the

administrative, executive employees registered even greater ratios than those in the professional and technical category.[20]

The same study also found that 'skill shortages prevailed in the carpentry and masonry, steelworks and welding, as well as in the plumbing and pipe-fitting categories.'[21]

In fact, the total demand for foreign as well as local labour exceeds the available skills in the professional technical and agricultural sectors, and in production-related work — all of which are crucial to economic performance.

An equally important and rarely recognised feature of labour migration is the fact that significant numbers of Filipino overseas workers lose their skills.[22] A survey conducted by the Institute of Labor and Manpower Studies (ILMS) revealed that more than two-thirds of the workers reported that they had not acquired any new skills in their overseas employment, and it is obvious that many of the college graduates and professionals who are working as domestic helpers in Hong Kong, Singapore, the Middle East and Western Europe are wasting their training and are unable to use their often considerable skills.[23]

Local industry is thus expected to function with a reserve army of unskilled and unemployed workers, who must fill vacancies left by those who are employed overseas. It is expected to bear the cost of educating and training new staff while the labour-importing countries do not contribute towards the resources which have been invested in the skilled people they employ. In fact, they pay Filipinos and workers from other developing countries significantly lower salaries.

Local industry spent on average about 2,000 pesos per person on training in 1978. Adding this to the cost of educating migrant workers, Manolo Abella, of the Institute of Labour and Manpower Studies, has estimated that the Philippines loses more from the drain in human experience and skill than it 'earns' from remittances. According to Abella, the value of educational capital embodied in Filipino migrant workers who left the country between 1975 and 1977 amounted to about 3.7 bn pesos. [24]

In 1981, when the exodus of workers reached its peak, the investment was far greater, of course — perhaps as much as 1.6 trillion pesos.

The real cost of training, moreover, is much higher than the simple cost of education. It costs some 5,000 pesos to train a blue collar worker in the construction industry, for example.[25] Even if the loss proves to be temporary, and we suppose trained workers will return to work in the domestic economy, the industrial sector and the national economy will not recover the full cost of their investment in these individuals. There are other indirect costs as well — for education, manpower development and social programmes. Finally, the Philippines loses the possible contributions these workers would have made towards the country's development. It is no wonder that many social scientists regard the labour export programme and its attendant costs to the country as Philippine aid to the developed and newly industrializing countries for their progress and their development.

127

The export of Filipino labour does not make a desirable or positive impact on the Philippine economy in general. The idea that it brings in much needed foreign exchange to offset the monetary crisis and fuel economic growth is only partially correct. While dollars from workers' earnings are undoubtedly used to service loan principal and interest, cushioning the negative impact of the country's perennial balance of payments deficit, the money has not been productively used. In the Philippines, it is a myth that income from remittances leads to domestic capital formation. It is also false that labour export has solved the problem of unemployment. In fact, the labour export programme harms the domestic economy by siphoning off skilled workers who cannot be replaced and who have a crucial contribution to make to the country's economic development. At present, the Philippines is losing its most precious skills, and shortages are already evident in important sectors of the economy. To make matters worse, many of those working abroad are not even acquiring new skills, contrary to the wishes of the government, but becoming 'de-skilled'. However many dollars and cents are earned from the labour trade, the long term costs incurred by the country are likely to outweigh any benefits.

NOTES

Chapter 1: Feelings of Loss

1. *The Effects of International Contract Labour*, Integrated Research Center, De la Salle University, Manila, Philippines. Mar 1983. Vol.I Eds: Stella P. Go, Leticia T. Postrado, Pilar Ramos-Jimenez; Vol.II Eds: Josefa S. Francisco, Pilar Ramos-Jimenez. Vol.I, p105.
2. *Op.cit.*, Vol.I, pp105-106.
3. *Op.cit.*, Vol.I, p.209.
4. The De la Salle report compared the cost of sending contract workers abroad with the average total remittances received by households over a six-month period (Peso 7,651 per household). *Op.cit.*, Vol.I, p.106.
5. *Op.cit.*, Vol.II, p.70.

Chapter 2: History

1. Luis V. Teodoro (ed.), *Out of this Struggle: The Filipinos in Hawaii*, 1981, p.3.
2. Edwin T. Fujii & James Mak, 'The Effects of Acculturation and Assimilation on the Income of Immigrant Filipino Men in Hawai', *Philippine Review of Economics and Business*, Vol XVIII, Nos. 1 & 2, March and June 1981, p.75.
3. B.Lasker, *Filipino Immigration to the Continental United States and to Hawaii*, Chicago, U. of Chicago Press, 1931. Reprinted by Arno Press and the New York Times, 1969.
4. For a vivid fictional description of this era, see Carlos Bulosan, *America in the Heart*, Harcourt, Brace & Co., (New York) and National Book Store Inc. (Manila).
5. Institute of Labor and Manpower Studies, *Working Abroad*, ILMS, 1984, p.9.
6. National Economic and Development Authority, Philippine Development Plan 1978-82.

Chapter 3: Government Regulation of Labour
1. National Economic and Development Authority, *Philippine Development Plan 1978-82.*
2. Charles W. Stahl, *International Labour Migration and the ASEAN Economies,* Working paper, ASEAN-Australian Economic Relations Project, p.15.
3. Arnel de Guzman, in Fr. Anthony Paganoni (Ed.), *Migration from the Philippines,* Manila, Scalabrinian Fathers, 1984, p.129.
4. See the provisions of the 1974 Labor Code, and Central Bank circulars 364 and 534.
5. Kaibigan, *EO 857, Filipino Overseas Workers' Remittances — the Multi-Billion Dollar Question,* 1983, p.3.
6. *Op.cit.* pp3-5.
7. Appeal, 21 January 1985, signed by 13 Filipino organisations in Hong Kong and supported by nine Hong Kong organisations.

Chapter 4: The United States
1. Ron Takaki, *Pah Hana: Plantation Life and Labor in Hawaii* (Honolulu: University of Hawaii Press, 1983), pp55-56.
2. Luis Teodoro, tr., ed., *Out of this Struggle — The Filipinos in Hawaii* (Honolulu: University of Hawaii Press, 1981), p.19.
3. Ruben Alcantara, 1981, quoted in Fred Cordova, *Filipinos: Forgotten Asian Americans* (Seattle: Demonstration Project for Asian Americans, 1983) p.30-31.
4. Alberta Alcoy Asis, quoted in Cordova, *op cit.,* pp32-33.
5. Ruben Alcantara, 'American Subcultures: Filipino-Americans,' 1975, pp59, 70.
6. Alcantara, *op cit.,* p.78.
7. Alcantara, *op cit.,* pp75-76.
8. Alcantara, *op cit.,* p.106. Much of our discussion of the contrast between California and Hawaii Filipinos is taken from Alcantara.
9. Alcantara, *op cit.,* p.107.
10. Josephine Romero Loable, Salinas, California, quoted in Cordova *op. cit.,* p.41.
11. H. Brett Melendy, 'Filipinos in the United States,' *Pacific Historical Review,* XLIII:4 (Nov.1974), p.528.
12. Vince Reyes, 'Second Wave Immigrants — Enter the War Brides,' *Ang Katipunan,* XI:3 (March 1985), p.12.
13. Jesse G. Quinsaat, 'How to Join the Navy, and Still Not See the World', in *Letters in Exile,* UCLA Asian American Studies Center, Los Angeles, 1976, p.107.
14. *Op cit.,* pp107-108.
15. Teodoro, *op cit.,* Chapter 3, 'Lessons in Organization: Filipinos and the Labor Movement', pp19-25.
16. Howard A. Dewitt, 'The Filipino Labor Union: The Salinas Lettuce Strike of 1934,' *Amerasia Journal,* V:2 (1978), p.1.
17. Venny Villapando, 'How the 1940's Red Scare Victimized U.S. Filipino Labor Leaders', *Ang Katipunan,* VIII:12 (December 1982-January 1983), p.8.
18. Melendy, 'Filipinos...,' *op cit.,* p.532.
19. It is, of course, impossible to document or even reliably estimate the 'TNT' portion of the community. One instructive set of figures might be the number of Filipinos entering the U.S. as non-immigrants. From 1971 to 1975, the number

averaged 57,000 per year. This number steadily grew until it reached 101,000 in 1978. (US Immigration and Naturalization Service, 1984). How many of these people chose to remain as illegals is anybody's guess. Impressionistic evidence indicates, a lot!

20. Manola Abella, 'Cost and Benefits of Exporting Filipino Manpower,' typescript, p.2.
21. Mike Davis, 'The Political Economy of Late-Imperial America,' *New Left Review*, No. 143, Jan-Feb 1984, pp6-38.
22. Edwin Almiral, *Ethnic Identity and Social Negotiation: A Study of a Filipino Community in California*, unpublished Ph.D. dissertation, Department of Anthropology, University of Illinois at Urbana, 1977.
23. California Health and Welfare Agency, 'An Ethnic Profile: Filipinos in California,' December 1982, summarized in *Ang Katipunan*, March 1983, p.8.

Chapter 6: Europe
1. Maggie Burns, London, Commission for Filipino Migrant Workers, 1984. *Filipinos in Camden*, Embassy figures quoted in report.
2. *Royal Anthropological Institute News* (RAIN) survey conducted in 1979.
3. J. Nash. 1980. *Filipinos in Britain*.
4. Catholic Committee for Racial Justice, *Notes and Reports*, April 1980.
5. Leila Maw, 1974. *Immigrants and Employment in the clothing industry: The Rochdale Case*, The Runnymede Trust.
6. Migrants Action Group, 1982. *On the Road to Repatriation*.
7. Commonwealth citizens were British subjects, but also citizens of their own countries (India, Jamaica etc). Only people from British colonies were still UK citizens.
8. Unpublished research by Clare Demuth for the Migrants Action Group on the functioning of the work permit system under the immigration law.
9. This rule was changed following a ruling by the European Court of Human Rights, to which three test cases were submitted, including one concerning a Filipino. Nevertheless, women now have to be settled in Britain, prove they can provide accommodation and will not have recourse to public funds, and show that, in marrying, it was not the husband's primary intention to enter the United Kingdom. The last condition is particularly hard to satisfy if there is a challenge.

Useful addresses in Britain
The Filipino Chaplaincy,
18 Gunnersbury Crescent, Acton, London W3.
Tel: 01-992 9347.

Pagkakaisa ng Samahang Pilipino (United Filipino Association),
49 Connaught Street, London W2 2BB.
Tel: 01-402 6917

The Commission for Filipino Migrant Workers (CFMW),
St Francis of Assissi Centre, Pottery Lane, London W11.
Tel: 01-221 0356

Philippine Resource Centre,
1/2 Grangeway, Kilburn, London NW6 2BW.
Tel: 01-624 0270

Chapter 7: The Middle East
1. 'Oil for Underdevelopment an Discrimination: the Case of Kuwait', by an observer, *Monthly Review*, Nov 1978, *passim*.
2. Charles B. Keely, 'Asian Workers Migration to the Middle East', Jan 1981,

Geneva, pp45-46.
3. Housewife in 'Biyaya ng Saudi' (Saudi Benefits) by Rene Emaas, *People's Journal* 24 Sept 1983, p14.
4. *Business Day*, 15 March 1983, p2.
5. Vivien T. Supangco and T. Lorenzo Pastor, 'Overseas Employment: an Overview', *Manpower Monograph*, Vol 2, June 1982, *passim*.
6. POEA, 'Preliminary Report, January-June 1983', POEA Ministry of Labour and Employment, p3.
7. 'Survey of the Needs of Dumez Filipino Overseas Workers', Dumez Company, Philippines, 31 July 1982, p1.
8. Regina B. Dacanay, 'Work Conditions of Contract Workers Abroad', *Philippine Labour Review*, Second Quarter 1981, Vol 6, no.2, p45.
9. 'Overseas Employment Programme: A Policy Analysis', POEA, MOLE, Philippines, 1982, pp41-42.
10. Estrella A.Consolacion, 'Katas ng Saudi Labo Report: A Summary', from *The Review*, October 1982, *passim*.
11. 'Mideast Fiasco Faces Probe', *Bulletin Today*, September 1983.
12. 'The Stranded Workers of Carlson Al Saudia', *Financial Times*, 18 Sept 1982.
13. *Bulletin Today*, Manila, 16 Nov 1984.
14. 'Survey of the Needs of Dumez Filipino Workers', *op. cit.*
15. Supangco, *Loc. cit*, p6.
16. 'Overseas Employment Program: A Policy Analysis', *Loc cit*, pp41-42.
17. Supangco, *Loc. cit*, p6.
18. *The Review*, Oct 1982.
19. 'Promoting Welfare of RP Workers in Saudi', *Daily Express*, Manila, 9 March 1982.
20. POEA 'Rules and Regulations Governing Overseas Employment', MOLE, Philippines, 1983, *passim*.

Chapter 8: Asia-Pacific Region
1. V.G. Kulkarni, 'Young, rich and eligible', *Far Eastern Economic Review*, 26 Jan 1984.
2. *The Filipino Maids in Hong Kong*, Mission for Migrant Workers: Hong Kong, March 1983.
3. *The Filipino Maids in Hong Kong*, *op cit*.
4. *Filipino Workers: Off to Distant Shores*, Mission for Filipino Migrants Workers, Hong Kong, 1983.
5. Andrew Hicks, *Filipina Domestic Helpers in Hong Kong*, University of Hong Kong, March 18, 1982.
6. *Ibid*.
7. *The Filipino Maids in Hong Kong*, *op cit*.
8. *Ibid*.
9. *Ibid*.
10 Ma.Alcestis Abrera-Mangahas, *An Evaluation of the Philippine Overseas Employment Promotion Policy*, Quezon City, 1984, pp55-100.
11. 'Exploitation of Pinoy Entertainers Abroad: The Show Must Go On?', *Skills News*, March 1984.
12. *Asia Today and Women Who Work in Foreign Countries*, a report by the Japanese Delegation in a women's consultation by the Christian Conference of Asia held in Maryhill Retreat Centre, Manila, Philippines, Sept 1984.
13. 'Initial Survey on the Filipinos in Japan', unpublished report, 1984.

14. *Bulletin Today*, 26 Aug 1984.
15. *Ibid.*
16. *Asiaweek*, 9 Nov 1984.
17. *Sunday Times*, Manila, 5 Aug 1984.
18. *Daily Express*, Manila, Aug 1984.

Chapter 10: Macro-Economic Effects
 1. Stephen Castles, Heather Booth and Tina Wallace, *Here for Good,* Pluto Press, London, 1984, p.l.
 2. Speech delivered by President Ferdinand E. Marcos at the First National Congress on Overseas Employment, 20 July 1982, PICC, Manila.
 3. *An Analysis of the Philippine Economic Crisis, A Workshop Report,* prepared by Dante B. Canlas, *et.al.*, U.P. School of Economics, Quezon City, June 1984.
 4. *Op cit.*, pp25-26.
 5. Roberto D. Tiglao, 'Payment on Foreign Debts, Interests to take up 52% of Export Earnings', *Business Day*, 6 August 1984, p.2.
 6. Stella Go, Leticia Postrado and Pilar Jimenez, *The Effects of International Contract Labor*, Vol. I, Integrated Research Center, De La Salle University, Manila, 1983.
 7. Cited by Ma. Alcestis Abrera-Mangahas from *OEDB 1976 Annual Report* in her essay 'An Evaluation of the Philippine Overseas Employment Promotion Policy', as compiled in *Migration from the Philippines* by Fr. Anthony Paganoni, Scalabrinians, Quezon City, 1984, p.76.
 8. Mangahas, *op. cit.*, p.78.
 9. An estimated 600,000 people join the Philippine workforce annually.
10. Manolo Abella, *Export of Filipino Manpower*, Institute of Labor and Manpower Studies, Ministry of Labor and Employment, Manila, 1979, p.53.
11. Philippine Overseas Employment Administration 1983 Annual Report, p. 10.
12. *HR Magazine*, p. 7.
13. Canlas, *et. al., op. cit.*, p.36.
14. *Ibon* No. 91 from a 'Special Report on the Profile of Filipino Overseas Workers,' Office of Emigrant Affairs, MOLE, 1981; OEDB Annual Report 1980: 'The Philippine Overseas Employment Program,' April 1980.
15. *Employment and Travel Tribune*, 'Skill Drain Feared as Exodus Continues,' Vol.I. no. 1, 22-28 Feb 1982, p. 5.
16. Resolution No. 6, The National Conference of Employers IV, Makati, Metro Manila, April 1983.
17. Rodrigo V. Alvarez, 'Skilled Workers "Outflow Curbed",' *Business Day*, 15 July 1980, p.1.
18. Alvarez, *op cit.*,
19. Cited by Ma. Virginia Sinay-Aguilar, *et.al.*, from Patricia Sto. Tomas, 'Overseas Labor Migration,' Discussion Paper for the Fourth National Population Congress, 1981 in their work *Outflow of Scarce Skills in the Philippines, 1975-1982* Research and Publication Program, Institute of Industrial Relations, University of the Philippines, Quezon City, 1983, p.4.
20. Ma. Virginia Sinay-Aguilar *et al.* p. 41.
21. *Op. cit.*, p.52.
22. *Op. cit.*, p. 4.
23. *Op. cit.*,
24. Abella, *op. cit.*, p. 60.
25. *Op. cit.*,

INDEX